Life
Doesn't Come With
Instructions:

A Guide for Successful Living

by Dennis Pezzato, PhD.

Buonsenso Press
Cambria, CA

For information please write:

Buonsenso Press
Dennis Pezzato
P.O. Box 1434
Cambria, CA. 93428
U.S.A.

Or visit Dennis' Web site at
www.dennispezzato.com

Life Doesn't Come With Instructions:
A Guide for Successful Living

All Six Books in the Series

Acknowledgements

The unending support of my wife, Paula, continues to be a cornerstone of my journey. Dr. Donald G. Burger continues to be my mentor, validator, and the brother I never had. Special friends support me, and those whom I may have helped inspire me.

No one who is fortunate enough to realize and live their purpose and passion does so without the loving support and help from others.

Preface

None of us were born with a set of instructions and maps that we might be able to use at some time in the future.

Many of us have trouble understanding who we are, and what our roles are in life. Most of us have lots of questions about how to best fulfill some of those roles.

How do we deal with money? How does money affect other areas of our lives? How do we choose a mate, or plan to marry? How, once we have a mate, do we deal with children? How, once those children have grown into adults, do we relate to our adult children?

There can be so many questions, and at times too few answers. Life really is a trial and error proposition, isn't it? Perhaps, by being open to some frank and sound information, we can increase our odds of having more success at life's roles and in attaining greater skills.

We Don't Come With Instructions:

A Pocket Guide To Understanding Ourselves

by Dennis Pezzato, Ph.D.

Buonsenso Press
Cambria, California

Table of Contents

Preface

Life, for each of us, really is a solo journey. There is no reliable method that each of us can employ to guide us through the process of learning about ourselves and our place and purpose in life. Since most of us are unsure about what makes us tick, it is beneficial to take a closer look at ourselves in ways we may not have done before. Life's journey can be more interesting and fulfilling if we can develop a deeper understanding of ourselves. Other significant advantages of self discovery are deeper insights into our relationships with the people around us.

Learning how to improve is a huge advantage for getting to know ourselves. How much have you thought about most of the decisions you make? Do all of us just react and respond based on our evolving beliefs and values without any self- directed analysis? How do we determine what to expect of ourselves? How do we monitor ourselves, if at all? Do we question ourselves before, during, or after a decision? If so, what do we ask ourselves? Do we accept our answers, or do we continue to question? How often do we bring significant others into this process? How much do others influence how we think, act, and believe?

These are some of the questions and ideas I discuss in this book. The content is brief, to allow you ease and flexibility in taking in the information. I believe that if you give serious reflective thought to understanding yourself better, the effort may help you to become a more sensitive and worthwhile person. Isn't that the important goal each of us has in life?

Introduction

My purpose in writing this book is to share with you my opinions and ideas about how to understand and get in touch with yourself; and to do so in a way that will benefit you, and allow you to enjoy yourself on your individual journey. I believe that by gaining a greater understanding of ourselves, we also gain a greater understanding of others. Understanding is the basis for acceptance, and acceptance can promote a more peaceful and harmonious existence for all of us.

How to Utilize this Book

This is not intended to be a how-to book or an all-inclusive text. I pose questions and share opinions and concepts for you to consider. It is my hope that you will evaluate what is stated and formulate your own views. I suggest that you have conversations with your spouse, close family members, and valued others whom you feel would be receptive to honest and open mutual introspection. I strongly encourage you to make use of a personal journal in order to write your thoughts down. Putting down on paper what you normally keep in your mind allows you to transition from the more abstract to the more concrete. Writing it down allows you to see a clearer picture and refer back to that picture at any time. I also encourage you, after reading this book, to follow-up with other books written by experts in the field. Add to your education about yourself in any way you can so you can attain a clearer understanding of the process of self-awareness and personal growth. When you have finished reading this book, please see the list of suggested readings at the back of the book. I have chosen these books because they may benefit you in ways that will increase your understanding of yourself and others.

Where Do We Begin?

It is important to understand that we begin the process of self-awareness at some point after conception and again immediately after birth. Why do I think we have two beginnings? Because after we are conceived, the process of growing and evolving from basic cellular structure, to an entire personage occurs in a self-contained world, which is the womb. The mother provides the safety and sustenance that is the womb.

Once born and released from that cocoon, this new person enters a totally different and uninsulated environment; one filled with new forms of stimulation and challenge. It is a dependable certainty that most, if not all of the newborn's needs, will be met by loving parents. But who really understands what all of these needs are? As infants, we cannot have a conscious awareness of our needs. Parents can only attempt to discover by trial and error what these needs are. Difficult as it may be to relate to this early time of life, those early months and years with little or no verbal communication have a significant affect on the developing personality, which is formed during this period. Once verbal communication comes into play, we all relate more comfortably to the importance that communication plays in a child's development.

The Early Years

The point of discussing this early period is to help the reader understand that the experiences encountered by us during this time span have a profound affect on determining who we are to become. By age two or three, we have already been subjected to more satisfaction and disappointment in our early lives than any of us have ever given much thought about. Also, during this early period, we mature from doing things naturally with uninhibited behavior, such as pooping in our Pampers, to learning how to control our functions. For all intents and purposes, we learn to exercise control to please our parents (the potty-trainers).

From this time forward, we spend our childhood and adolescent years developing, learning, adjusting, resisting, pleasing; ever-changing as unique human beings. We cannot conceive of the numbers of experiences and changes that occur over the first two decades of life. We become a personal receptacle for all that we have seen, heard, smelled, touched, tasted, and thought.

As we progress through each stage or phase of development, we formulate thoughts, ideas, and feelings about our own identities as well as the identities of others who have influence in our lives. We constantly compare our view of ourselves to reactions and opinions of others. We are social creatures who develop an ongoing sense of who we are from others as long as we live.

While our personal experiences are formative, there is another facet of our personalities that shares equal responsibility for who we become. This is composed of the traits we were born with. These traits come from our genetic imprint and predisposes us to certain behavior patterns and tendencies. We are born with a certain type of temperament, with certain intellectual capacities, and with a variable level of pre-programming. So, just as you may look a lot like a parent or relative, you may also get your musical abilities from one or more of the persons in your ancestry. So we become who we are, at any point in time, as a result of what we inherit through our genes which is modified or enlarged by our life experiences.

Self-Definition

How do we define ourselves to ourselves? How do you really know who or what you are? This question has been asked by men and women as long as there has been life on earth. Many of us require a definition that will serve as a personal guide to our human condition and enable us to describe our separate individuality and our purpose. Obviously, the answer for each of us must be subjective. Just as there are many facets that make up a diamond (and we are more complex in nature), so to are there many facets that define us. And there are just as many ways to examine ourselves from different perspectives. The purpose of this book is to help you find ways to look at yourself and discover some of the facets that make you who you are, and which you have not appreciated..

When you try to look at yourself, do you see a person who has self-love, self-esteem, self-confidence? Do you feel worthwhile, valued, needed, lovable, and loving? Or instead, do you see yourself as a person with little self-respect, unloving or unlovable and who does not feel valued, needed, or worthwhile? Or, do you see in yourself some of the assets listed above, but which are undeveloped?

Once you have defined who you are, and what kind of person you perceive yourself to be or wish to be, then it is time to take a personal inventory of your assets and liabilities. In the next section there are questions to be answered that will help you compare your initial self assessment with how it may change when you have answered the questions.

Personal Inventory

This inventory has been devised to elicit an honest response from you about what you believe are your strengths and your weaknesses, as well as your major traits, tendencies, likes, and dislikes. This may be a difficult exercise for some of you, so here are some recommendations to assist you in the process. Remember to take your time with this exercise. Quiet, alone-time is the best setting without distractions. Be honest with your answers; the only person who will read them is you, unless you wish to share them. Write out your answers so that you will have them to refer to.

The sample personal inventory below may nudge you with ideas to create your own list. The purpose of the sample is to get you started. Do your best to answer these questions with a Yes or No (Y/N):

- I am a nice person
- I am honest
- I am unselfish
- I am loving
- I am lovable
- I am likable
- I am hardworking
- I am considerate of others
- I am thoughtful
- I am sincere
- I am sensitive
- I am open-minded
- I am patient
- I am caring
- I like animals
- I am environmentally responsible
- I am fair
- I am intelligent

All of the above would be considered strengths or desirable traits by most of us. The opposites of those in the list would be considered weaknesses or undesirable traits, which can be improved when you acknowledge them. And, of course, that is the purpose of a personal inventory — to describe who you believe yourself to be at a given stage in your life and determine how to improve on it, if you so choose.

The other beneficial aspect of a self- inventory lies in the value of the process itself and the ever-changing discoveries of connecting with yourself. As an aside, this personal inventory, when completed by each of a couple who are contemplating marriage, can be used effectively as a tool in assessing compatibility.

Now What?

Now that you have completed your personal inventory, you are probably asking yourself "What do I do now?" I suggest that you use the information to decide whether or not you are pleased with the picture you have described. If you are pleased, then move forward on your journey with a new awareness; continue in the direction you are going. However, every one of us could make improvements to himself or herself. Think about striving to grow and expanding in new directions. Do this for yourself and for the benefit of others. As we grow and improve, we become more valuable to ourselves and to the relationships we have.

If you are not pleased with the picture you have painted, then perhaps it is time to figure out what changes you are willing to make. Change does not come easily, especially if you feel it comes with too big of a price tag. I happen to believe that positive personal growth and the accompanying change, benefits us far beyond any price we pay to accomplish that change.

Shopping List

If you desire to change your view of yourself or alter your behavior, you need to refer to your personal inventory and determine what it is about yourself that you don't like, and want to improve upon. We can accomplish changes by becoming aware of the need, but we should be fair to ourselves in the process. Rome wasn't built in a day and neither were you. So be patient and make the changes you want for yourself step by step, one day at a time. Remember if you are overly critical, you may expect too much too quickly, and give up because the effort is too great.

Let's say there are some things you've identified that you should improve upon. What's next? First, you need to make a written list of the changes you wish to make or the attributes you want to acquire. If you write them down, it will be easier to organize your thoughts and your plan of action. Most of us have an understanding of what we and others respect, admire, and feel are positive and negative attributes. If you need guidance in the change making you wish to accomplish, ask the opinions of people you value, or seek advice from clergy or professional counselors.

For the most part, I believe that when a person gets to this stage he or she knows what is desirable, but may not have a clear understanding of how to make the changes happen.

Making Change Happen

The quality of every experience in life is a function of how we view that experience. We can choose to view it in a positive or negative light. Change can be implemented much more rapidly and effectively, as well as with greater ease, if it is done with a positive attitude focused on the ultimate growth change can bring.

If you are going to make some changes, choose to take a positive approach, have an attitude of excitement about the new possibilities, and formulate a plan for how you intend to get to where you want to go. Write the plan down, study it once, and then again. Does the plan make sense? Does it seem workable? Is it too ambitious, or not enough? Will it get you to your goal? If you aren't sure, put it aside for a while and come back to it later. Spend the time away to ponder and mull over everything. Sleep on it if necessary. Then reread your plan and see how you feel. If you still don't feel comfortable, then it may be time for you to enlist the help of a loved-one, friend, or professional who can be honest and supportive.

Once you are comfortable with your plan to implement change, pump yourself up with positive self-talk, and get excited about what you are about to do. Jump in with both feet and have fun with it. What do you have to lose? Making permanent changes are not accomplished in an emergency frame of mind. Your plan is not a test; you cannot fail. Just put forth the effort, and the outcome should please you in some way. If, after a reasonable period of time and effort, you really are not satisfied with the result, then make adjustments. Making changes in yourself is like creating a work of art; you are the artist and you can create what you want. Do so, and be happy about the improvement no matter how small. Little steps still make a mile, and the accomplishment seems more solid and satisfying when it is not rushed. You need to trust yourself and realize that you have the power within yourself to create and make change happen for yourself.

Flying Solo

Life for each of us really is a solo journey. No matter how we are connected to others, and to what degree we are intimate, each moment we exist is being experienced as a solitary soul. Although we may share many aspects of our lives with loved ones, friends, and others, we share every breath, thought, and all of our senses with only ourselves. You are never as intimate with any human being as you are with yourself.

It may seem as though I am pointing out the obvious but I do so to make a further point. You must make yourself your top priority in your life. Please yourself first, and then please others. This is not a selfish attitude because there are many times when we place our needs behind those of others. When I suggest pleasing yourself, I mean taking responsibility for aspects of your life: physically, psychologically, emotionally, spiritually, and intellectually. If you love, respect, and nurture yourself, you will be better prepared to treat others in a nurturing supportive way.

The Right Equipment

You may ask yourself at this point if you are really equipped to participate in life in the ways you would like. Are you equipped to make an honest personal inventory? Are you ready to make changes in order to become more fulfilled and at peace with who you are, or will be. My answer to these questions is an unequivocal "Yes." You have the ability to accomplish whatever it is you want to do. I believe without hesitation that each one of us has the basic intelligence and mental faculties to accomplish great things — with the possible exception of those who are severely challenged mentally or physically,.

We may not always be prepared properly to accomplish everything we desire, but we can learn what it takes to prepare ourselves. We need only to be patient, determined, flexible, adaptable, and willing to work hard. No one is born in the place where they end up; we all must take our individual journeys. With standard equipment and adequate preparation, anything is possible.

Self-Directed or Other-Directed

Inside most of us is a bundle of desires to do and to be many different people. We experience many different roles every single day. When you look at yourself from the perspective of who you are and what you do, you may observe that you are not always moving in the direction of your choosing. This probably means that you are not self-directed, but other-directed — moving in directions others choose for you, or that you think others want. We all have a need to please, a need that began in early childhood.

If you choose to defer to others to gain approval, acceptance, and value, you may betray your inner self. Consequently, you spend much of your life doing things, and assuming roles counter to your own deep-seated desires. This does not mean that the influence of others cannot be of significant value. On the contrary, you do not live in a vacuum; you need the influence and assistance of others in life, but you must learn to weigh and interpret how the views of others may influence you adversely despite good intentions. Chart your own course by confirming and acting on the motivations that best express the desires compatible with what your heart, mind, and gut tells you. For many of us, a self-directed course can be difficult, and takes practice. But remember, what we practice most in life is what will become habit.

A Journey of Choices

I am convinced that everything we do and think, are choices we make. I am also convinced that our choices of thoughts and actions are a product of our own psychological need for love, acceptance, freedom, personal power, gratification, and security. Many of you may not have given much thought to this premise. Most of us, I believe, feel we have fewer choices than we would like, and we are controlled by too many forces in life that are difficult to resist.

Granted, during childhood our choices are limited because our parents dictate our behavior. In adolescence, even though we can make more choices for ourselves, we are stifled by parental rules and we believe we can't do anything we want to do. Then comes lingering adolescence blending into early adulthood. This surely is a time of independence, of leaving the nest, a time to cut loose. But then we encounter still too many controls, too many people to answer to, and we feel over controlled.

Adulthood comes next, and we get married, settle on a career, have a family; truly a time of greater independence, a period in which we call the shots and make our way with our own choices. But then we are burdened by different pressures. Is there ever really a time when we are truly independent to make the choices that please us? Probably for most of us the answer is: no, not really.

If you believe you are a victim of circumstances, then you may be held prisoner by that conviction. I believe we make conscious and unconscious choices during every waking hour, as well as unconscious choices we're not even aware of. Certainly, we make plenty of concessions and considerations in our course through life. But only you can evade the trap of "expected behavior" by choosing a different course for yourself, as many successful men and women have done. They do not accept who they are expected to be. They build a different picture of themselves in their minds and adapt themselves to make the picture a reality.

You can do the same thing and discover that true independence is a gift to you from yourself.

Behavior and Consequences

Our behavior, which can be defined as our thoughts and actions, is a product of the choices we make. We decide, for whatever reason, to act or behave in a certain way. We act out this model hundreds and thousands of times every day. We choose to get out of bed, brush our teeth, smile, say "good morning", eat breakfast, dress a certain way, buy a particular car, drive at certain speeds. We are constantly choosing our behavior. The end result of our chosen behavior is a consequence of the action. There are times when we have no control over the consequences, but we have almost total control over our behavior. If you are very lucky, you may have learned this truth while you were growing up. Your parents may have taught you this valuable lesson at an early age (smart parents).

My purpose in addressing this subject is to remind you that if you pay more attention to this aspect of your human functioning there is a strong probability that you can make your life journey, and your relationships more productive, positive, rewarding, and less stressful. Take care with the behaviors you choose. The consequences of those behaviors can be to your immense benefit, or to your detriment.

Giving Is Getting

On the subject of behavior, there is one aspect that is remarkably rewarding and its consequences to you predictably result in unexpected returns to you that will change your life in ways you cannot conceive. Giving is what I'm talking about — giving because it makes you feel good. Giving to others is one of the most rewarding experiences in life. In fact there is research to support the theory that giving can be beneficial, both physiologically and psychologically. The positive emotions which accompany true, selfless giving and doing for others, can actually trigger the release of chemicals in the body that benefit it and the mind. This is not voodoo; this is real.

Giving is such magical and wonderful behavior. It is magical in the sense that so many positive things can happen as a result. When we give to another person, that person benefits in some real or concrete way, but that person also benefits in abstract ways as well. The recipient of your love and giving also feels better, feels valued, and feels important. Chances are that person may go on to do something for someone else — a reciprocal effect that may ripple through to many others.

At the very least, the receiver will feel good for a time. And, as if that were not enough, you the giver, will feel good about what you gave. That feeling of goodness cannot help but affect your mind and your body in a positive way and cause you to have a more positive attitude. Your new attitude will, for a time, affect other relationships. We need to understand that as social beings with all sorts of relationships, our attitudes influence our states of mind, our behaviors, and ultimately all of our relationships, and they rub off. Giving, and the accompanying feelings of grace and generosity have the potential to change many things in our world. On the other hand, taking without reciprocation, without caring and sharing, can have a detrimental affect on us, others, and our world.

Self Acceptance

Are you your own biggest fan? I think you should be your number one fan, cheerleader, and proponent. Many of us may be reluctant to say we either like or love ourselves. Granted, many of us can be difficult, unlikable, unlovable, full of faults, and the like, but should that really get in the way of basic self-love? Let's face it, none of us is without faults because we are human. To be human is to be fallible, vulnerable, fragile, and imperfect. But we all have special and unique qualities and strengths. We all have unlimited potential to be any kind of person we choose to be. We have more potential than we realize or give ourselves credit for.

Within each of us, at levels which may vary in degrees of consciousness, resides unique attributes which we must explore and utilize for our own sake and the sake of others. As we become more aware of our strengths, we will increase our resolve to use and build on those strengths, and allow them to override our weaknesses. We can direct our strengths to be our dominant feature of self-identity. We can allow them to motivate our behavior. There is no good reason not to accept ourselves as is, knowing that we are who and what we are, or who and what we can choose to change in ourselves to make us more acceptable.

There is so much more to be gained from viewing ourselves from a positive perspective with a spirit of loving acceptance and tolerance, than from a negative perspective full of disdain, doubt, and lack of love. Within each of us lies a spirit of peace, love, and acceptance. It benefits us and those to whom we relate, if we can connect with what lies within; then share it with the world.

Purpose in Life

It seems as though there has been much discussion in recent years about Purpose in life; do we have it, should we have it, how do we define it or find it? Perhaps I have become more aware of this issue because I have recently rediscovered and acted upon what I believe to be my purpose in life. The idea of purpose has become more prevalent in the last few years. A simple explanation for this is that we have evolved to the point where life has become so overwhelmingly complex and difficult for so many that we've begun to question ourselves and our basic values. We are not as happy as we feel we ought to be. We have progressed so far we are over-stressed, running constantly, and not really happy.

I think many of us need more self-definition and spiritual enhancement in our lives. The idea of purpose can be seen as a means of centering oneself in more solid values. But purpose can be illusive and difficult to define, as well as being a very subjective entity. Purpose is individual and people are learning that it is an "absolute necessity." How else can a person define herself or himself without a destination that purpose leads the individual to?

Purpose, for me personally, has been necessary because the germ of it has resided in my mind, heart, and soul since my boyhood. It was below the surface most of the time. It wasn't until my 57th year that I rediscovered and connected with how that purpose was to manifest itself. When that awakening occurred, there was no doubt about what I had to do with the rest of my life. I knew I must devote it to helping others. The way I chose to fulfill this purpose was by writing and speaking about issues of human behavior we all struggle with every day. For some of us, purpose can be as dramatic as a clear "calling". For others, it can be as simple and undramatic as the way in which we choose to live our everyday lives. If you feel you need to find a purpose, my advice is not to look too hard or exhaust yourself in the search. Show purpose in living each day with love and respect for yourself and others. Try to see and appreciate the best in yourself; and make giving, a central theme in your life. I believe we were born with a general purpose of loving one another. Allow life to happen without forcing things, and you may discover less of a need for a dramatic and all consuming purpose. You may come to realize that you are already living the purpose that suits you and makes you real.

Religion, Spirituality and Tolerance

At the risk of offending some people, I am compelled to say something about the importance of society's acknowledgement of the existence of a Higher Power. I think that some form of religious teachings, organized or otherwise, some form of spirituality with a sense of community is absolutely key to our ability to function as social beings. For many of us the ideal of a Golden Rule, "Do unto others," was first experienced through some kind of religious epiphany.

For much of mankind, a person's faith in a God or a Higher Power is what gives us the religious teachings can help give us a moral code by which to live. Most religions teach a for our fellow man.

Lacking any religious or spiritual connection, we owe it to ourselves, our loved ones, and each other, to adopt and maintain an attitude of tolerance and acceptance of other human beings. We are a universal family, and as such we must learn to live together in peace. If we do not find and share that spirit within ourselves, then I am afraid we fail ourselves and we fail others as well.

Responsibility

Fulfilling one's own needs without interfering with another person's ability to fulfill his or her needs is one definition of responsibility. We are not born responsible individuals. We have to learn acceptable behaviors to demonstrate our individual responsibility within the cultural boundaries of our environment. Doing so also involves interactions with others as we pursue personal fulfillment. Our most basic psychological needs are to love, be loved, and to feel needed and worthwhile. In order to love, be loved, and be considered worthwhile by others, we must prove ourselves worthy of trust and demonstrate suitable aspects of behavior which are considered responsible.

Once we have learned the basic differences between responsible and irresponsible behavior, we are then able to choose how to act in a culturally approved manner. Maintaining a satisfactory standard of responsible behavior is a struggle for some. I believe that our struggles relate primarily to our upbringing, our childhood, and our adolescent years. Many parents do not agree with or understand the importance of the use of love, discipline and structure in the raising of their children.

Whatever our processes of learning in the past, we can learn new behaviors by changing the current behaviors that seem not to be working for us. With the right attitude and motivation, every old dog can learn new tricks as a means to become more responsible and more fulfilled.

Attitude

At the risk of sounding crass, let me say that statement probably elicited a reaction by most of you that was negative, at least momentarily. But it is actually a very true statement when worded in a slightly different manner: we all possess attitudes about everything in life. Our attitudes of thinking, feeling, or acting. The sources of our attitudes are cultural, familial, and personal. We can be influenced by so many sources which include the media, social authority, business, education, and any number of entities which seek to influence social conduct.

We are constantly processing the information we experience and as a result form opinions and develop our attitudes. All of our behavior reflects these attitudes. We can choose to have a good or positive attitude through which we can see things with an open mind and a warm heart, or we can choose to have a bad or negative attitude through which we see things with a closed mind and a cold heart. Which type of attitude do you think will give you the most rewarding life experience?

Attitude colors the way we see things, the way we experience things, and also has an affect on our physical being. Attitude can reward or punish the body without us even knowing that it is happening. We choose our attitudes, just as we choose our behavior.

Opportunity

Oh boy, do I love this one! I try to see opportunity in just about everything I do! I adopted that philosophy after hearing a motivational speaker, Zig Ziglar in the late 1970s. He referred to the typical alarm clock as an "opportunity clock". Since that time I have always tried to keep that positive perspective. Opportunities are everywhere for all of us if we choose to look for them and act on them. By simply being alive, we have endless opportunities to enrich our lives and the lives of others. Too many of us get bogged down in everyday life. We settle for less from ourselves, less from others, and less from the world. If you expect to enjoy life and find many sources of gratification and fulfillment, then you must not only participate, you must seek opportunities to expand your involvement and experiences.

Remember the discussion about attitude? Well, you have to adopt the attitude that you really can find opportunity for growth and fulfillment in almost anything you experience. There is much information, and there are many lessons to be learned if we are willing to be open and receptive. Life itself is our opportunity.

Goals and Plans

For many human beings survival, simply staying alive, is the goal of a lifetime. But for the majority of my reading audience survival is not an issue; you have lots of goals that may or may not be recognized as such. We all have wants and needs that we try to have satisfied, either by others or by ourselves, or by a combination of both. Most of the time we are probably not consciously aware that what we do to satisfy our most basic needs and wants, is a process of setting and achieving goals. We are more aware of goals when we are attempting to achieve something out of the ordinary that may require extra planning and effort. Sleeping, eating, playing, learning, working, plodding along in a general fashion seems mundane and almost non goal-directed.

I contend that these acts are all goal- directed toward self satisfaction. The goals that I want to address are the kinds of goals we all need to have if we truly want to become the person we either see ourselves to be, or would like to become; the our purpose in life.

My theory is that in order for you to understand what your goals are you need to work through some of the issues already addressed earlier in this book, as a means of better understanding yourself. Once you have a clearer picture and sense of self, it should become easier short, medium, and long-term. You may have very ambitious long-term goals that require lots of effort and time; the best way to achieve those lofty goals is to break the process down into many short or medium-term goals first. As you move forward (always move forward and keep moving) and success-fully reach and meet the shorter-term goals, you will build confidence, awareness, and a success-oriented attitude; these are stepping stones to your ultimate destination of reaching that long-term goal.

However, in order to reach any goal, you are best served by having a plan. You wouldn't just take off across the desert or any other place you've never been without a plan, a map, and enough provisions to see you through to your destination. Achieving goals in life is no different. Make a plan, review the plan, and then embark on the journey. If that plan doesn't work for some reason, modify it based on what you learned that did not work the first time; then try it again. Eventually you will find a plan that will work for you, and you will achieve your goal. Congratulations, you should feel proud of yourself. Now you can move on to the next goal, knowing what success feels like. Goals in life are important, they help to make us feel alive and they fuel our feelings of self-worth and self- respect. Remember to always be considerate of others while in pursuit of your goals and dreams. Set goals and have a plan, you will enjoy the journey.

Whose Goals?

If one of your goals in life is to become more in touch with who you really are as a person, and to live life in a manner that you feel is true to who you are, then it is important to recognize whether you are striving to fulfill your own goals or the goals someone else has set for you. Are you pleasing yourself or someone else? Many of us let family, friends, and others define who we are or what we should be. Many of us are directed by expectations others have of us. Perhaps our parents pushed us in a direction, albeit with the best intentions, into a career or a relationship. Perhaps a spouse and/or the pressures of having a family push us in a direction we feel obligated to go toward, but would really rather not pursue.

There are many influences in our lives that have more control over us than we either recognize or are willing to admit. Make sure you are being true to yourself; make certain that the goals you set are your goals and not someone else's goals for you. Try to recognize the difference and make a choice, understanding full well the potential consequence of fulfilling someone else's goals.

Fear and Uncertainty

"Join the club" is a phrase I've heard all my adult life from other adults. It is usually used in response to someone who is complaining about something in either a joking or serious way; the listener will respond by saying "Hey, join the club". The meaning of the statement is that you are not alone in your situation; many of us have the same problem.

When it comes to experiencing fears and uncertainty on aregular basis in our lives, it is part of human existence; we are in the same club. Because we are living, social beings with intellect and free will, there is no escaping this natural state of feeling. Just as we cannot really know "good" without knowing "bad," we cannot know "certainty" and "fearlessness" without feeling "fear" and "uncertainty". Fear and uncertainty are one of the earliest experiences we have in our lives; and to some degree they will always be with us. They are really assets, tools with which we learn to protect ourselves from harm. They are a means by which we gain courage, knowledge, and self-confidence. Don't deny these feelings in your life. Instead, accept them and welcome them to whatever extent possible, as learning mechanisms which aid personal growth. Use them to gain a better understanding of yourself. Hey, join the club!

Self Trust

When we experience fear and uncertainty, which is probably a daily occurrence at some level, it usually involves our relationships with others, or with events in the world outside of ourselves. Often as not, these threatening and intimidating feelings are caused by a lack of trust and confidence in ourselves. We all have an inner voice which is a combination of body and mind that communicates with us about what we are experiencing, or about what we are about to experience. Some refer to this as intuition, gut-feelings, or inner voice. All of us possess this quality in varying degrees. It is a tool that is not only meant to be used, but should be developed further for greater use.

We all need to trust ourselves more. I acknowledge that there are those of us who may be confused, immature, maladaptive, underdeveloped, developmentally and psychologically challenged. For those individuals, their journey in life is much more challenging, but no less rewarding. For the vast majority of us, however, there should be no doubt that we are more knowledgeable about ourselves than anyone else; we are more intimate with ourselves than anyone else can be. We live within ourselves and our existence. We know our own identity, we know how we feel and think, both physically and emotionally. So, who better to put your trust in than yourself? Listen to what your inner voices yourself to do what is best for you.

Besides, what do you have to lose? Really! If you trust yourself and act on that trust, the worst that can happen in a non life threatening situation is that you miscalculate the outcome. If that happens, you try something else. But in the process you will have learned a lot about yourself (the internal) and something about others and the world (the external). Be yourself by trusting yourself.

Balance

The dictionary defines balance as a state of equilibrium, and as mental and emotional stability. In order to get the most out of life, it is critically important to have mental and emotional stability. We can achieve this more often if we keep most aspects of our lives in a state of equilibrium. Without balance we are constantly struggling to move in too many directions and serve too many masters. In the process, we waste too much time, energy, resources, and we do a disservice to ourselves. An unbalanced life is an unhappy life.

I believe we must deal with both internal balance, which is how we function mentally and emotionally, and external balance, which is how we go about living our lives. Both are extremely important and influential on each other. If either is out of balance a lot, the other will likely suffer a negative consequence.

In order to stay mentally healthy, we must maintain a balance between conflicting needs, desires and responsibilities. If we are to strive for and accomplish balance in our lives, we absolutely must learn discipline. Discipline is a form of self-control that we use as a tool for successful living. Let's face it, life is a series of problems that require solutions, and we are constantly making adjustments in order to cope. Discipline is what we must learn in order to successfully cope with those problems. Problems bring us pain and discomfort that must be confronted. Problems evoke in us many anger, anxiety, loneliness, guilt and regret. In order to mature and continually grow, we must experience the suffering that accompanies dealing with our problems. Discipline allows us to be flexible in our approach. It is what empowers us to say "yes" or "no" at the appropriate times in order to solve problems, minimize pain, and strike a balance between pain and pleasure.

Pleasure is easy to deal with, but too much of it can put us at risk to experience more pain. How can this be? you might ask. I am convinced that when we take things to excess, we risk incurring pain caused by extreme forms of behavior — behavior that may cause us to neglect other aspects of our lives that need our attention, but which may be suffering because we are so consumed by indulging in a particular pleasure.

By contrast, not enough pleasure creates more pain as well. Too little pleasure can cause resentment toward our duties and responsibilities. Resentment causes anger and pain. Balance is at best a successful juggling act between wants and needs. The more we are successful at achieving balance in all areas of our lives, the more at peace we will be to experience our lives in ways that are in harmony with who we really are as individual human beings.

Love

I must admit some reluctance about discussing love because of the difficulty in attempting to define what love is. I don't know if there can ever be a generally satisfactory definition of love. Love is so many things, and in many ways a mystery. However, I do have some thoughts about what love can be to many of us, certainly for me. Love is the will to give of oneself in an unselfish, nurturing way in order to celebrate and sustain your own, and another's life. To feel love requires very little, or so it may seem; and the desire to love is not love itself. Love is a conscious act of will; it requires an intention as well as an action or behavior. As with all behavior, we have a choice in what we do, how we act. Real love then, is a choice to act. Love requires demonstrable effort along with personal judgment. You might be asking why judgment enters into the process of demonstrating love. The reason judgment is important is because when we choose to express our love by our actions, as we must, we need to exercise good judgment over what actions are appropriate to our love goals, and which are not.

During this process we are constantly torn by decisions to give or withhold, praise or criticize. An example of a wrong demonstration of love might be the giving of material things instead of your time and attention. An example of the right demonstration of love might be displays of affection and sensitivity to another's needs. The goal should be for our demonstrations of love to be contributing to nurturance and growth.

Never forget that real love, by any definition, has its beginning within each of us. We cannot and will not be able to love others in a real sense, without learning to love ourselves first. Self love is a prerequisite to other love. Just as giving attention and listening to others is at the center of demonstrating love, so too is attention and listening to yourself at the center of your self love. Love is giving, so choose every opportunity to give. Love is life's fuel.

Solutions

One thing we all have in common as human beings is that we have problems, almost always. Problems come and problems go. They can be minor or major. They can be brief or they can be ongoing. We can be the source of our own problems or those of other people. Whatever the kind of problem, or whatever the source, one thing is certain, we usually feel the need to get rid of our problems. What is the best way to go about finding solutions to our problems, especially the nagging, painful, stress-inducing kind of problems that can consume us to the point of affecting our physical and emotional health?

The first thing I suggest is to step back and try to take a closer, more objective look at things. Is it something external over which you have no control, or is it something internal, over which you do have control? If it is internal then perhaps you can adjust your attitude and perspective. This first step is usually the most difficult one because the tendency most of us have is to have an instant solution. We want instant gratification and are not into waiting patiently for things. We have to be willing to delay gratification by learning and using self-discipline in all aspects of our lives, not just problem solving. Problems won't go away by themselves, they must be confronted and worked through so that they do not become barriers to personal growth. The ability to solve problems promotes personal development and growth.

Getting back to finding solutions, the next step after identifying the problem is to brain- storm how to solve it. Write down the possible ways to deal with the problem in a head-on manner. At the top of your list please write, "I have the right equipment to solve the problem. The second thing you should write on your list is, "I will be patient; I will not be in a hurry. I will persevere. I can, and will do this."

Once you've completed your list, and it feels reasonably workable, move forward to implement your problem solving plan. Many things in life involve a trial and error process. Problem solving is one of those things. If your first approach does not produce satisfactory results, try an other approach, and another, and another until you are satisfied with the solution.

This whole issue of problems and solutions is all about attitude. Remember our discussion about attitude earlier in the book?

Accept that life presents us with a never ending series of problems, and they are actually a necessary part of life. Adopt a willing attitude to see your problems as tools for learning and growing and as opportunities to build character, confidence, and a spirit of joy in the pursuit of life's pleasures and opportunities.

Multi Tasking

I don't have a lot to say about multi tasking but I do want to give you a little food for thought. It seems to me that multi tasking has taken on a heroic connotation in our current highly technological, highly competitive, and fast-paced existence in America. I get the sense that having the ability to multi task, both at work and at home has become a badge of honor, something to brag about and aspire to. Quite simply, I think that is not good for us. As a world, as a nation, and as a society, we may have progressed and evolved technologically in many areas, but we have not progressed and evolved as far psychologically. I do not think we can expect our minds and our emotions to be able to function like computers.

I think multi tasking can cause a short circuit in our brains, minds, spirits, and bodies. I think we need to slow down some things to a more manageable pace. We do not have to buy into and get caught up in every aspect of "the fast pace of life." Keep in mind that I am not referring to all forms of multi tasking, such as talking while driving a car, talking while cooking or doing the dishes. Personally, I can usually "walk and chew gum" without stumbling. I think you get the picture.

I do not think, on the other hand, that you should put on makeup, talk on the cell phone, and drive your car 70 miles per hour on the freeway. Slow things down; life is not an emergency. Nowadays, for too many of us, smelling the roses is not an issue; just seeing the roses at all, is the real problem.

Anger

Anger is a natural emotion and feeling it is as much a part of being human as breathing. We all have experienced anger in all of its many forms and disguises since birth. We begin life concerned with only one thing, self-gratification. From birth, most of us have almost all of our basic needs provided for us by parents and care-givers. However, when we sense something is not quite right, we express our displeasure by crying, screaming, kicking, and fussing. We learn quickly that by doing those things we can usually have our needs met by someone; almost anyone will do, as long as we, who are at the center of the universe, can be satisfied and comfortable.

Later, as we enter early childhood, we discover we are no longer considered helpless. From that time forward, we have demands placed on us. As we experience these demands, we also experience the frustration and anger which accompanies not having our demands met; we do not like being held accountable.

We spend our entire lives trying to have our needs met; trying to get our way. It is not only a matter of getting our way, it is also complicated by complex matters of fairness, hurt and injustice insofar as how we are treated by others. Any number of situations and events can trigger an angry reaction within us. It is important to understand that anger is a real and necessary emotion. It is unpreventable, which does not mean it is uncontrollable. It is also important to understand not only the source of our anger, but how to express and process our anger in ways that are not harmful to us or others.

We should accept that anger is part of life. It does, after all, reflect our disappointments when ideas or beliefs we cherish are trampled on or unfairly criticized. Make it a point to under- stand that anger as a guardian of our personal values is a built-in monitor, but uncontrolled or chronic anger can harm your body and your relationships with others.

Stress

Stress is as difficult to define as love. Interestingly, stress plays as big a role in our existence as does love. Stress, in and of itself, is not really bad or good. It is a component of our natural "fight or flight" instinct. It is a natural mechanism that enables us to respond to challenges in life. When we encounter stressors, or situations that are challenging, we automatically switch to a higher level of alertness, consciousness, and focus. We respond with a certain level of stress. That level can be positive or negative. The positive form of stress allows us to control the stress. In so doing we build confidence and feel empowered while successfully dealing with whatever the stressful situation is. On the other hand when we respond with a negative level of stress, that negativity prevents us from controlling the stress. When stress is uncontrollable, it produces negative consequences (more later on negative consequences). So consequently, the belief that we have control seems to be an important key to stress management.

The stress that seems to be uncontrollable is the stress most of us think about when we discuss it in our lives. We probably seldom think that stress can be positive. So let's focus on the negative aspect of stress. Stress is an inevitable part of our existence. It also plays a key role in our overall physical and psychological health. Chronic stress can cause physiological changes that can cause health problems. Many diseases are either caused by or made worse by stress. Things like cancer, heart disease, migraine headaches, ulcers, back and spine problems can all be caused or made worse by negative stress. So how do we prevent stress from contributing to ill health?

I suggest two things: one, that we learn stress management techniques, and second, that we learn to eliminate some of the stressors in our lives. Both of these options may prove difficult for many of you, but are necessary if you are to accomplish a goal of optimum health and enjoyment in life.

In discussing the elimination of stressors, it is important to assess what your stressors are, and whether or not it is practical or possible to modify or eliminate them. I would suggest as a first step, going back to some of the previous chapters in this book to formulate a clearer picture of yourself. See the chapters on Personal Inventory, Making Change Happen, A Journey of Choices, Attitude and Balance. Once you've done that review, you may have a different perspective on yourself and what you can accomplish, Now, why don't you consider which stressors can be removed. What situations and circumstances in your life can you avoid or not participate in?

Next, you have to be completely honest with yourself, while considering the short and long term effects of your decisions. If, after careful consideration, you cannot eliminate any of the stressors in your life, or if after removing some stressors, you still are having difficulties, you must learn how to manage the remaining and ever changing stressors you will encounter. This is called coping.

Coping is a process of stress management that changes constantly. The two basic coping approaches are: One, we use our minds and our emotions to change how we view the stressors in our lives. Two, we learn to cope by developing our problem-solving skills (see chapter on Solutions). Personally, I have by necessity, learned to use both coping strategies simultaneously. The first strategy, which is to view stressors differently, works well as long as you don't stick your head in the sand and live in denial. Don't try to trick yourself into adopting a new view without a strong foundation of thought. To develop a new view you need to reason out, and believe the new view honestly. My personal favorite is problem solving because it tends to build confidence.

Finally, let me say that you are the best resource available for effective coping strategies. I believe that after gaining some new personal awareness through books like this one, you can commit to taking the best care of yourself. Good physical health, maintained through exercise and proper nutrition, a positive attitude, good social support, a belief in yourself and the choices you can make to empower yourself, are all things you can do for yourself; things that will benefit you and your coping strategies. So go out there and cope!

Mind-Body Connection

In my opinion, the purpose of understanding the connection between the mind and body is not one of satisfying curiosity, but one of survival. By survival I mean just that, surviving all that life throws at us and all that we impose on ourselves. More importantly, I believe that understanding the mind-body connection will improve your overall quality of life and the practice of wellness principles in your life. Wellness constitutes overall good health, not just the absence of disease. Until recently, our health care system has focused mostly on making ailing bodies well, without reference to the dominance of the mind. Instead, as many caregivers know, we should be treating individuals as a whole - body and mind.

It has been reported that over the past 50–100 years, the major causes of death have changed from diseases which were contagious, to those which were not. Most modern diseases are those identified as cancer, heart and lung disease, hypertension and diabetes. Modern diseases are basically lifestyle diseases, with the exception of some hereditary illnesses which may explain some predispositions to certain physical problems. There now exists a field of psychology called health psychology, which is the study of the relationship between psychological behavior and physical health and illness; the emphasis is on wellness and prevention.

Many healthcare professionals believe that the immune system is at the center of our physical health, and when it is compromised or suppressed, the body becomes more susceptible to breakdown and disease. Stress plays a huge role in negatively affecting the immune system, making us vulnerable to modern disease. I believe that wellness is all about lifestyle and behavior, insofar as our own ability to have control over this aspect of our health and wellness. Obviously other factors beyond our control affect our state of health. These are influences like genetics, environment, sex, age, bacteria and viruses.

But I believe the greatest detriment to our physical or mental health is stress. I will not discuss stress in depth here, but only refer to it. For more on stress, please read the preceding chapter.

My purpose in this chapter is to help you create an awareness of your own mind-body connection and what you can do to help yourself progress toward a greater level of self-control over your personal health and wellness. First and foremost, you must understand the role that stress plays in your life, then assess the extent to which it really affects your health. Next, you need to eliminate your stressors wherever possible and learn to manage the stress you cannot eliminate. Beyond that, there are other things you should look at as resources to help you deal with life on a daily basis. Your resources are things like your personal level of health and energy. You must participate in beneficial levels of exercise, diet, and relaxation. I am going to digress briefly to suggest that relaxation is critical; relaxation can be comprised of leisure-time activities, alone time, meditation or prayer, deep and controlled breathing, other natural relaxation techniques, and adequate rest.

In further discussion of resources, do you have a positive attitude and belief system with which you view life and health? You also need to learn and practice social skills that contribute to positive, fruitful, and productive co-existence with others, in all types of relationships. We all need to develop a circle of social support which will accompany us on parts of our life journey. Two resources are perhaps the most effective, if not the most important. First, you have to exercise personal control over yourself and understand that you have a choice in everything you do. You have the ultimate say so over your mind and your body. You have ultimate control over what drives and motivates you in your daily life.

Having a compelling purpose can literally provide the magic elixir, that unknown entity ultimately contributes to a healthy mind and spirit, and every fiber of my being that Giving is the key to having a purpose in life and is the key to creating and sustaining the highest levels of optimum mind-body health. Giving is materials, giving is an attitude, giving is compassion, understanding, acceptance, tolerance, and love. The mindset we have by living these forms of giving will be a gift to ourselves as well as to others; a gift to our minds and our bodies.

Whether you believe it or not, whether you like it or not, your mind and your body are inextricably connected. Learn to listen and respect both. Do so and the rewards will be endless.

Spirit

Spirit, like love and stress, is another of those terms hard to define. My thoughts about spirit is that it is the essence of a person's true self. On the surface, most of us appear to know who we are, or at least we tell others as much. However, I believe that most of us are not really in touch with our true selves, though we wish to be. How, then, do we learn about ourselves? We do so by "feeling" our responses to the experiences, physical and mental which we have. As we process feelings, we also experience the purpose behind, or in, the event that produces the feeling. As we continually pass through new feelings, we learn more and more about ourselves.

Unfortunately, we frequently feel stifled by the world around us which interferes with our need to be ourselves, unhindered by outside influences. We have learned since childhood the social skills we require to function in society. Often the exercise of these skills interfere with the practice of self-expression. Nevertheless, as we move forward in the ongoing, never-ending process of self discovery we can sense a deep connection to our core as individuals. "Who I am is what I feel and believe because it seems natural and right at any given time."

I think it is important to understand that this is a process and a journey that continually moves and changes. Just as every part of our body changes during every moment of life, so too do our thoughts and feelings. Therefore our definition of self can change and evolve. As each growth as an important element of becoming closer and closer to your true self. Embrace and share your spirit, it has much to offer you and the rest of us.

Human Relationships

It is my belief that relationships in life hold the keys to much, if not all of our personal happiness and mental health. We owe it to relationship possible with our spouse, family, friends, and those with whom we share our life experiences.

We can choose to be givers who demonstrate, through behavior and actions, our caring willing to receive demonstrations of love and caring from others without demonstrating the sensitivity of the reciprocation. A valuable relationship is based on mutual effort and understanding. The more each person understands the other's motivation for his or her actions, the easier it will be to coexist. The more understood a person feels by another person, the easier it will be to make adjustments, changes, and concessions that will aid in creating a more mutually satisfying and harmonious relationship.

Grab Bag Items

Mirror, mirror on the wall, who do I see? When you look into the mirror, beyond your physical appearance, you may see your parents or other family of origin members. You may see past personal history, some pleasant memories and some not so pleasant. You may see strengths or weaknesses; you may see faults and virtues. The list of the things you might see when you look closer and closer could be endless. What I think would be inspiring for you to see is a truly special human being, one with talents, strengths, and values. One who has unlimited potential to reach out in many directions in life. I believe each one of us has that potential. Do yourself and the rest of us a favor and look in the mirror for the person you really are and can be.

In all aspects of life and in all your relationships, especially the relationship with yourself, try not to react too quickly to situations that occur. Develop a personal "Hold" button. think before you act. This will allow you to consider an appropriate response rather than a hasty reaction. We tend to react before we think, much more frequently than we are aware. This pause will become an enabler of control within you. Practice this technique often, it really works.

Conclusion and Overview

For the majority of us, introspection is probably not something we spend a lot of time at; it is very likely uncomfortable or foreign as well. Perhaps some of us are contemplative by nature, and do delve into our deeper levels of being. Others maybe content with the attitude that "we are what we are; what you see is what you get;" and "everything is just fine the way it is." But I think the majority of us, if we are honest, would admit to struggling through life in more ways than we would like.

I want to do everything I can to help others prevent avoidable struggle wherever possible. My goals are to help others understand themselves in ways that will help in the development of new attitudes about themselves and others — to develop new coping skills, and build a greater sense of self-empowerment and spirit.

It is through increased awareness and understanding that we learn, grow, and flourish in life. Be open to taking the time to look deeper and longer at who you are, and what you are capable of, beyond what you currently believe. Learn to celebrate life, living, and the opportunity for giving — to yourself and to others. Share your spirit.

Suggested Reading List

Sound Mind, Sound Body, Dr. Kenneth Pelletier

Get Out Of Your Own Way, Mark Goulston, M.D. andPhilip Goldberg

Life Strategies, Dr. Phil McGraw

Self Matters, Dr. Phil McGraw

Healing The Child Within, Charles L. Whitfield, M.D.

The Power of Empathy, Arthur P. Ciaramicoli, Ed.D., Ph.D. and Katherine Ketcham

On Becoming A Person, Carl R. Rogers (Textbook)

Psychology in Action, Karen Huffman (Textbook, 6th edition)

Money Doesn't Come With Instructions:

A Pocket Guide To Personal Financial Behavior

Dennis Pezzato, Ph.D.

Buonsenso Press
Cambria, California

Table of Contents

Preface

It seems as though an awful lot of people in the United States have money problems. By that I mean that many people don't have enough money to pay all of their bills; more money going out than there is money coming in.

I get the sense that two of our most prevalent trends in American society are that we are perpetually broke and/ or overweight. Why do I mention being overweight in a book about money? Because while pondering this problem, it occurred to me that there is a connection between being fat and being broke. If we spent less money on the wrong foods and getting over-weight, we would have more money for other things in life that would help us enjoy our good health and well-being. Another thing that occurred to me, relative to being broke and over-ßweight, is the behavior relationship the two problems have.

In dealing with being overweight, the formula is simple: balance is achieved by equalizing "calories in" with "calories out". That means you maintain balance or healthy weight by burning (by exercising) as many or more calories as you take in. On the other hand with the issue of money, balance is achieved by not spending (exercising, burning) more than you earn. While being overweight is a major problem in our society, I will not address that problem in this book. However, I will just say that an overweight condition is not solved by diet or food alone, any more than money problems are solved by more money.

These are both behavioral problems. We behave our way into debt just as we behave our way to obesity.

INTRODUCTION

You don't solve money problems with more money. My purpose in writing this book is to share with you my opinions and ideas about personal behavior which has led to personal financial problems. I believe that by gaining a better understanding of our personal behavior, our place in society, and the world around us, we can make adjustments and changes that will lead to better choices in life regarding our financial behavior.

How to Utilize this Book

This is not intended to be a how-to book or an all-inclusive text. I pose questions and share opinions and concepts for you to consider. I want you to evaluate the validity of what is stated and formulate your own view. However, it is important that you try to keep an open mind and be brutally honest with yourself about your beliefs and behaviors. I encourage you to seek the advice of a family member or friend whom you trust; a person you know has succeeded in achieving financial balance and stability in his or her life. This friend may be able to communicate with you about managing money in a way that makes you comfortable. Allow that person to read this book as well, so that you can discuss these ideas together.

Getting yourself educated about money management in a way that enables you to attain a clearer understanding of the processes involved in how we relate to money and how we behave in our financial matters is important. When you have finished reading this book, please see my list of suggested readings at the back of the book.

In the Beginning

Who we are and how we behave is based on two strong influences: on our genes (those we inherited) and on what we have learned. Most of what we learn comes from our families of origin and the local environment of our upbringing as well as our exposure to the predominant culture and the world, plus exposure to the mass media.

We spend all of our pre-adult years soaking up, sorting through, and filtering information about everything in life. As independent adults, we make decisions based on the beliefs we created while processing all that information we were exposed to; and we continue to process new information and make adjustments in our beliefs and values unless we stop learning.

What we learned and how we view or interpret it determines how we choose to behave. This may be productive or destructive. It is really pretty easy to determine which of these applies at any given time. Just ask yourself if what you are doing is working for you. Are you safe and secure or not? Are you in trouble or at risk of getting into trouble or not? If the answers are negative, then you must take a close look at what beliefs and behaviors brought you to where you are. In order to understand the present, it is usually helpful to look to the past.

Get a Grip

Sometimes in order to get a grip on what we are doing and where we are going, it is wise to take some time to assess where we've been that a good way to do this is to schedule some solid quiet time alone on a daily or weekly basis; preferably more than an hour at a time. Try to get yourself in a frame of mind to be honest, open, organized, and eager.

This should all be done in writing — long hand, with no computer. Use whatever kind of paper, cardboard, corkboard, or grease-board put your life on display (privately if necessary) so that you can view it all at a glance.

Begin by naming categories or aspects of your life such as, but not limited to, age, current life partner status, education, job, living arrangement (rent or own), income, expenses, debt, goals (short, medium, long-term), dreams, fears, children, commitments, hobbies, etc. You really want the most complete picture of your life in its current state. This will take some time, so be patient and try to enjoy the process. Once you are satisfied that you've got all of the information down that you can think of, begin the process of reading the story that this narrative tells you; let it soak-in and allow it to trigger thoughts and feelings.

Then you need to decide if you are pleased with what you see and whether or not you are comfortable with who and where you are. Then work on deciding where you want to go from here.

Taking Action

Now that you have a pretty good picture of where you are and where you want to go, it's time to take action. What action? What direction? How do I begin? What changes do I make, and how do I make them happen? These are all questions I will attempt to help you answer for yourself in subsequent chapters, but before we go in that direction, I would like to discuss some other facets of your life, and issues that play major roles in how, as a social being, you function. Be patient with me and with yourself in trying to understand how these issues apply in your life and in how you function, feel, and believe. The more you understand about yourself, others, and the world around you, the more comfortable it will be to make change and implement new ideas and goals.

A Journey of Choice

I am convinced that everything we do and everything we think, is a choice that we make. I am also convinced that our choices of thoughts and actions are a product of our psychological need for love, acceptance, freedom, personal power, gratification, and security. I doubt whether many of you have given much thought to this premise; and if you have, I expect many of you disagree. I'm certain most of you feel that you have fewer choices than you would like, but are basically controlled by too many forces in life that you simply cannot resist or control.

However, I disagree. I believe we make conscious and unconscious choices every waking hour of the day. I'm not saying there aren't plenty of considerations and concessions to be made with regard to others in our lives, what I am saying is that we need to think at a deeper level, about what choices we make, and how often we really could choose a different behavior if we really wanted to do so.

I believe for example, that we blame other people and circumstances for things we could have had a different choice about. Others give us information; we process the information and then decide what to do. We choose to be happy, sad, angry, worried, depressed, or whatever; or we choose a physical action to help others, be productive, be lazy, gratify ourselves in some way, spend money we don't have and create new or more debt. We make choices, always, in everything we do.

Responsibility

One definition of responsibility is that it is the ability to fulfill one's NEEDS in a way that does not interfere with the ability of another person to fulfill his or her needs. Once we have learned the basic differences between responsible and irresponsible behavior, we are then able to choose how to behave.

Learning to be responsible and maintaining a satisfactory standard of responsibility is for many of us, a struggle at times; and for some of us it is a constant struggle. I suggest that our struggles relate to three things: our upbringing, learned behavior in adulthood, and our drive for gratification. Recent generations seem to have little patience for earning, saving, and waiting for many of life's pleasures; many of us have poor impulse control and self-discipline. Not only can this get us into financial and relational difficulties, it can become habit-forming—a way of life. I consider this to be irresponsible behavior.

Balance in Life

The dictionary defines balance as a state of equilibrium, and also as mental and emotional stability. In order to get the most out of life, it is critically important to have balance. We can achieve this more often if we keep most aspects of our lives in a state of harmony. Without balance or equilibrium we are constantly struggling to move in too many directions at once. In the process we waste too much time, energy, and resources; and we wonder why we are not getting anywhere. An unbalanced life is an unhappy life.

In order to stay mentally healthy, we must maintain a balance between conflicting needs, wants, and other responsibilities. If we are to strive for, and accomplish a balance in our lives, we absolutely must learn discipline. Discipline is a form of self-control that we use as a tool for successful living. Let's face it, life is a series of problems that require solutions; and we are constantly making adjustments in order to cope. Discipline is required in order to successfully cope with those problems. Discipline is what empowers us to say "yes" or "no" at the appropriate times in order to solve problems, minimize pain, and strike a balance between pleasure and pain. Pleasure is usually easy to deal with, but too much pleasure can put us at risk to experience more pain. Very few things in life can cause us as much pain as money problems, especially the problems which are within our control.

Balance is at best a successful juggling act between WANTS and NEEDS. The more we are successful at achieving balance, the more we and our loved ones will live in peace and harmony.

Attitude

We all possess attitudes about everything in life. Attitudes are our predispositions to ways of thinking, feeling, or acting which show our dispositions and opinions. The sources of our attitudes are cultural, familial, and personal; and some of our attitudes are developed as adults, on the basis of our own perceptions and interpretations of our experiences. We can be influenced by so many sources: the media, public authority, business, educational institutions, and other sources that have influence over our conduct.

When it comes to our money-spending practices, the media has a hugely negative influence on us; playing on our desires for gratification and perceived status. We are constantly processing information that we experience. As a result of that process, we form opinions and develop our attitudes. All of our behaviors and actions are a result of out attitudes. Attitudes can color the way we see things, the way we experience things, the way we learn things. An attitude that is positive, open-minded, resistant to unimportant influences, patient, considerate, and caring will serve us best. Reject an attitude that is negative, closed-minded, selfish, impatient, and inconsiderate. Choose one that will allow you to be real about life and about your journey. Money is obviously a tremendously integral part of our lives and our culture. Our attitudes toward money and how we relate to it can determine how our use of it impacts the quality of our lives physically, psychologically, and spiritually.

Goals

For many human beings, survival—simply staying alive, is the goal of a lifetime. But for the majority of my reading audience, survival is not really an issue of great magnitude; you have lots of goals that may or may not be recognized as such. We all have wants and needs that we try to have satisfied either by ourselves, by others, or by a combination of both.

Much of the time we are not consciously aware that what we do to satisfy our most basic requirements is a process of setting and achieving goals. Awareness comes usually in the form of something we perceive as "a big deal" in our lives. Sleeping, eating, playing, learning, working, plodding along in a general fashion seems mundane and almost non-goal-directed.

These common everyday acts, I contend are all goal-directed toward self satisfaction. The goals I want to address are the goals that relate to money and your financial behavior. As with all types of goals, you are best served and more likely to succeed if you have a plan. You wouldn't just take off driving across the desert or any other place you've never been without a reliable vehicle, a map, water and provisions, money, and a destination. Achieving money goals is no different. You need to set your goal, make a plan based on gathering sufficient information, review your resources, provide a back-up or alternative plan, make sure you have a safety net (savings or emergency fund), and then move forward.

When money is involved, there may be greater risks and ramifications if you fall short or fail in the pursuit of a goal. Many goals in life require an investment of time, effort, and emotion but not really any money, so the consequences of failure in any form may not be devastating. However, failure in achieving money-related goals, may be felt for a longtime; and the duration to recover and rebound may influence other areas of your life in a negative way. You may lose self-confidence, get depressed, harm relationships, bring hardship to family members, or go deep in debt. There is a lot to consider when working toward your money-related goals. Pre pare and plan well so that when you choose a behavior, you are anticipating and prepared for the inevitable consequence, good or bad.

Whose Goals?

Are you alone? Do you exist in a vacuum? Do you have a partner? Do you have children or other family members whose care is in your hands? Are your goals connected to their goals and/or theirs to yours? Whose goals are you really working toward accomplishing; yours or someone else's? These are all questions you should ponder as part of your goal-setting process. This will help give you a perspective that may affect how you proceed and how you make decisions—how you behave.

When you are not flying solo but are connected to others who will in many ways, either benefit or suffer from your pursuit of money-related goals, you owe it to them, assuming they are adults, to make them part of your goal seeking. Help them understand what you are doing, who it will benefit, and what the potential risks are. If you are married or a life partner, always make decisions together.

Patience

Patience is not only considered a virtue, it can be the key to so many things in life; none more important than when you are involved in learning to manage your financial behavior. In no other time in our culture, of which I am aware, has a society as a whole been so impatient. We seem to be in a hurry about almost everything; we seek instant or immediate gratification in so many areas of our lives. I think that prior to the start of the so-called baby boom period, those born between 1946-1964, most people understood that one worked hard toward goals, earned, saved, and in time achieved some of their objectives. They were more patient about expectations of themselves and society. Nowadays, and in recent decades, we don't want to wait; we want it all now. We are not particularly tolerant or patient of any experience or process that makes us wait.

Learning and practicing patience in all areas of our lives, especially money and finances, will lessen stress, decrease the potential for many problems, and possibly increase your enjoyment and appreciation for what you have. We could all benefit from spending more time being positive about what we have, instead of being negative about what we don't have.

Stress

Stress, in and of itself is not really bad or good; it is a component of our natural "fight or flight" instinct. It is a natural mechanism that enables us to respond to challenges in life when we encounter stressors, or situations that are challenging. This is when we automatically switch to a higher level of alertness, consciousness, and focus. We respond with a certain level positive form of stress allows us to feel in control of pressures and feelings. In so doing, we build confidence and feel empowered while successfully dealing with whatever the stressful situation is.

On the other hand, when we respond negatively to stress, that negative response prevents us from controlling stress. When stress is uncontrollable, it produces unwelcome consequences that can affect the way we think, act and plan for the future. This is the type of stress most of us think about when we refer to it in our lives.

Money matters are one of the most common sources of negative reaction in our lives. Money affects our very existence, standard of living, and quality of life. What stress does not do, and should not do, is define who we are. Lack of money, no matter how patient and prudent you are, can cause stress in your life. This is a simple reality.

I don't intend to delve into stress and health-related issues in this book (see *We Don't Come With Instructions: A Pocket Guide To Understanding Ourselves*) but I do need to state that the best ways to cope with stress in your life are to eliminate and avoid stressors, the things that seem to cause personal doubts, uncertainty and anxiety, whenever possible. Learn stress management techniques. Two of the basic techniques I have found to be effective for coping or managing stress are as follows: One, you need to learn to use your mind and your emotions to change your attitude about the stressors in your life. Secondly, you should develop your problem-solving skills (see the next chapter on Solutions).

When it comes to money matters, the more knowledge we have (credible information), the better able we will be to understand how to this in turn can lead to reduced, and more manageable levels of stress caused by money matters and our accompanying financial behavior.

Solutions

Problem solving is a learned skill which can, and should be the object of continuous improvement as we grow and experience life. In learning and applying your problem-solving skills, remember to be patient with yourself and the process, and have confidence in the eventual outcome or solution. In order to find a solution to a problem you must first identify the problem. Once you have done that, patiently and methodically brainstorm on all the possible approaches you might take to solve the problem. These approaches should include what changes you can make that might make the situation better. I suggest you write down the possible ways there are to deal with the problem in a head-on manner; be brutally honest here. At the top of your list, write "I have the ability to solve this problem." Then write "I will be patient, honest, and I will persevere; I can, and will do this."

Once you've completed your list, and it appears to be reasonably workable, move forward to implement your problem-solving plan. Many things in life involve a trial-and-error process; problem solving is one of those. You may have to make adjustments in your plan in order to get the desired result. This whole issue of problems and solutions is all about attitude; remember our discussion about attitudes?

Accept that life presents us with a never-ending series of problems, and just as many solutions. They're actually a necessary part of our learning and growth process. Adopt a willing attitude to see your problems as tools for learning; as opportunities to build character, confidence, and a spirit of joy in the pursuit of life's pleasures and opportunities. You can choose to empower yourself to overcome any problem, money or otherwise.

Knowledge and Education

Education is all about information. We take- in information each day we are alive, and we process it based on our beliefs, goals, and attitudes. As we learn, grow, and mature we should become more selective and discerning about the values we place on certain information. In order to be responsible, we must choose to learn those things that will enable us to make sound, responsible decisions based on our level of acquired knowledge.

The more informed and educated we are both generally and specifically, the more chances of making choices based on sound judgment. If you are having money problems, and if your financial behavior history indicates poor choices based upon unsound judgment, then perhaps what you know about the use of money is inadequate. Obviously, one can have all the best information, education, and knowledge, but still use poor judgment in financial matters. In this case, knowledge isn't the issue; impulse control and poor judgment are likely to be the problems. What I am addressing here is the need for sound, credible information and education obtained from sources with proven approaches and techniques. These sources can be family, friends, financial professionals, and publications devoted to money management.

Get informed, get educated; build your base of knowledge; give yourself the best chances possible of succeeding in your goals.

Power

Power is all about the abilities we gain through the knowledge we possess, because of the education we take advantage of. This power translates into choices; the more we know, the more choices we have. This is how we empower ourselves throughout life. Power is not about superiority and domination. It is not about how much money we can make and spend. Once we realize where our true power lies, we must exercise sound judgment with a balanced perspective and a positive attitude about what we can accomplish with the money we have.

If You Are Married

When there are money problems within a marriage, whether there are children involved or not, each member of the couple and/or family suffers or is negatively impacted in some way; materially, physically, emotionally, or even spiritually. I will limit this discussion to just the marital influence on life partners.

A marital partnership requires 100% commitment and constant effort in order to grow, flourish, and sustain itself. The definition of partnership means that there is, or should be, an equalness and a fair togetherness. This attitude is healthy and necessary in order to prevent one or the other partner from feeling slighted or less important than the other. This does not mean that partners do not assume more or less influence or importance in different roles, and express different degrees of control at certain times; all of this done by mutual agreement.

Rather, partner equality means that each partner is one half of a whole, and of equal importance in life together, as well as relationship decisions. Individual decisions which are being made should always give consideration to the wishes, feelings, and sensitivities of both partners.

Regardless of who makes the money-related decisions, there needs to be agreement regarding the direction and goals you are working toward.

Money problems are usually considered among the top three most commonly fought-over and potentially destructive issues with marital partners; sex and children are the other two issues. If you are struggling with money problems, don't poison your relationship by allowing this to continue for even one more day. It is never too late to step back and take a new and fresh look at where you are now, and where you want to be.

Making Change Happen

Change, for any reason or purpose can be difficult. Change may be voluntary or involuntary. I think that however we perceive change, it is a form of growth; and growth is a good thing. The quality of every experience in life is a function of how you view that experience; you can choose to view it in a positive light or a negative light. Change can be implemented much more rapidly, with greater ease, and with increased productivity if it is done with a positive attitude focused on your ultimate goal.

So if you are going to make some changes, choose to take a positive approach; have an attitude of excitement about the new possibilities. Then, formulate a plan of how you intend to get to where you want to go. Write the plan down, look at it once, and then look at it again. Does it make sense? Does it seem workable? Will it get you to your goal? Have you enlisted the help of someone who has the proven ability to guide or advise you through the process?

Once you've answered these questions to your relative comfort and satisfaction, then pump yourself up and get excited about what you are going to accomplish. Jump-in with both feet (four feet if you are a couple) and make whatever sacrifices necessary to get you to a different place. You can make this happen! Get whatever help you need; don't let pride get in the way. You need to trust yourself and realize you have the power within yourself to create and do good things for yourself.

Money

Upon reflection, it seems so strange, how at times in life, money can be of such critical importance. And at other times it can be almost meaningless. It cannot buy some of the most important and the most meaningful things in our lives. There is a well-known financial guru, Suzie Orman, who always stresses putting people first before money and things.

I don't believe the old saying "money is the root of all evil"; that's like saying that "guns kill people". People kill people by using a tool (weapon) called a gun. We use money as a tool, as a means to an end. Money itself is not a problem, it is our use of money that can be problematic. Allow me to digress by saying that there are entirely too many people in our society who, no matter how hard they work and how careful they are, will always have money problems because they are at the lowest levels of the socio-economic strata. These are people who, for various reasons such as lack of education, unfortunate life-circumstances, lack of self-esteem and self-confidence, and too much misfortune, may never have enough for anything more than the barest of necessities because it simply costs so much too live in our country; and our country still has not seen fit to devise a system to take care of all of its less fortunate.

The desire for money and power gets in the way of the accomplishment of a more thorough approach to the humane treatment of everybody in our society. But that is all about behavior, will, empathy, and attitude. Yes, money rules our lives in many ways; yes money is very important. We need to be responsible and realistic where money matters are concerned, if we want to have more enjoyment and less self-inflicted stress in ourselves.

Material Possessions

I heard a quote once from Frank Sinatra, the famous singer/actor, who said that in life the person with the most toys is the winner. I don't know if he was serious or not, but that attitude sure does seem to be prevalent among a large segment of western culture.

In my 60-plus years, I have certainly observed that it seems to take more in material possessions to make people feel happy than ever before. Now, I will admit that part of my view may have been skewed by the fact that I came from poor and humble beginnings, described as the blue-collar, lower socioeconomic level. Eventually my family elevated itself to somewhere in the middle-class. However, I believe research would prove me not to be very biased about our seemingly insatiable desire for material gains, which, in many cases is taken to unhealthy excess.

The desire for self-gratification through materialistic pleasures may have become culturally acceptable, but it never has, and never will be what makes one really happy, fulfilled, and at peace as a human being. Don't misunderstand me, there is nothing wrong with having and enjoying nice things if you can afford them. We are all entitled to enjoy the fruits of our hard work in whatever ways we choose. The problem is that things get out of control when we become obsessed with the acquisition of "things", and this obsession causes us to have priorities in life that may not put people first, ahead of" things".

Another problem occurs when we act irresponsibly with regard to our spending habits while in pursuit of these things on which we have placed such value and importance.

Too many of us figure that if a few things make us happy and give us pleasure, then certainly "more things" will make us even important to keep a healthy, balanced and realistic perspective on the material things in life.

Consumer Mentality

This money issue is synonymous with the word materialism. Since the advent of television, more than at any other time in American history, we have been inundated by marketers trying to sell us something. They targeted the buying public (consumers) through television, convince us that we cannot live without a certain product. We would be better off if we bought such-and-such and we certainly deserve to have more modern conveniences, Our love-lives would be better if we used such-and-such. We mustn't be left behind by not being part of the "in-crowd"; etc., etc. I think you get the idea.

Well, guess what? We have bought into all of this—a bill of goods (no pun intended). I am not saying that there aren't lots of goods and services that benefit or please us in some ways; actually, we would find out about these things on our own without listening to all the advertisements, because word-of-mouth always spreads if something is good or bad. We, as a culture, have bought into this whole consumer mentality. Our desire to look, act, and feel accepted, attractive, and prosperous, etc., has put some of us onto a fast track of false self-perception and financial disaster.

Keeping up Appearances

"Keeping up with the Joneses" is a phrase I heard as a child growing up. It means that whatever you see your neighbors and friends have, you think you must have similar things, or better things. It also means that what we see in others as desirable, we may want to emulate. Of course this all ties into the consumer mentality. So many of us actually come to believe that we need to "keep up with the Joneses", even though we don't admit it or see it as such.

Let me reiterate that there is nothing wrong with having things and conforming materially to others, as long as you don't betray who you are as a person, or cause yourself or your family, financial difficulties because of it. I am not addressing lifestyle or standard-of-living, I am only addressing the kinds of choices we make, some of the motivation for those choices, and the possible negative consequences of that behavior.

What are appearances, anyway? Appearances are perceptions of what others see "on" us. I say "on" us rather than "in" us because what others see "on" the outside, or our appearance, is significant window dressing for the most part. It usually says very little about what is "in" us. We don't need to "keep up with the Joneses", that behavior can get in the way of helping you define who you are as a person; and it can cause you to be financially unrealistic and irresponsible. Be real about yourself and your money; and remember that the grass is seldom greener on the other side of the fence.

Credit Cards

Credit cards can help you sink or help you swim; and they can do that all at the same time. Consumer credit in general, and credit cards in particular, have been the bane of society's monetary compass. Going into debt is made far too easy, and too tempting for most of us to avoid. Most of us have too little financial education, and too much desire for instant gratification. That drive and desire is what credit card companies are capitalizing on.

Credit cards should be used as a tool; everyone could benefit from having at least one credit card for use in emergencies and/or business use. But the way we should be using our credit cards is by paying the bill in full when it comes, not by making partial or minimum payments at high interest rates. When you charge something on your credit card, you should already have the money saved somewhere in order to pay the bill; or you should be 100% certain you will have the money before the bill comes.

Credit cards are useful in emergency situations when cash, checking, and savings accounts are low or non-existent. However, you really do not want to get into the habit of using the "plastic" without back-up funds available. Everyone needs to have some savings for emergencies, so that you are not forced to pay the exorbitantly high interest rates most credit card companies charge. It would be better to borrow from family at an interest rate that would match or exceed their savings account interest, if that is an option for you. If you are fortunate enough to borrow from family, make certain that a payment schedule is set and agreed upon in writing; be a conscientious borrower.

When you get a credit card, choose one with a low interest rate (not just the teaser rate), with little or no annual fees; and some type of rewards/ rebate program. At the very minimum, shop around for the best interest rate, so that if you are faced with no alternative but to use the "plastic", you keep the cost of borrowing their money to a minimum. If you get into this position, remember to pay your balance off as soon as possible. Work more hours, spend less money, give something up for a while; do whatever you have to do to reduce and remove that kind of debt.

Budgeting

Budgeting is all about making a plan and implementing that plan. However, in order to formulate a plan, you must first understand what all of the elements of that plan need to be — the things that go into creating a budget. The first thing I suggest is that you prepare a realistic and thorough picture of your complete financial existence.

You will need to do this project in writing because you need concrete, graphic illustrations, all laid-out in front of you like a road-map in order to understand past, present, and future behavior which leads to choices and actions. You need to tell your financial story. You can do this on plain paper, lined paper, in a notebook, or (my preferences) on a giant surface like a map-size, a grease board, or a bulletin board. Any of these suggestions will enable you to see all of the information at a glance; I think it is easier to process things this way—when you see everything on one surface.

There are several categories of information you will need to put on your financial "story- board". You need to show yourself where all of the money goes; you should account for every whole-dollar as a minimum accounting of your spending habits. The categories are as follows: INCOME of any kind; job pay (gross and net), interest income from savings, gift money, gambling winnings, refunds of any kind, garage sale income, etc. EXPENSES of any kind, in any amount, and for any purpose. This is really the critical tell-tale part; do not leave anything out unless it is less than one dollar.

Housing (if you own, break this down into mortgage, taxes, and insurance), all utilities, food(groceries), food(eating out), gasoline, newspapers, magazines subscriptions, school or educational costs, doctor bills, charitable contributions, clothing, hygiene, haircuts, vacations, dates, coffee-to-go, entertainment, professional fees (legal, financial), home maintenance, dry-cleaners, laundromat, credit interest and fees, etc. As a sidebar, write down the interest rate for all loans. By now you should have a complete picture and a story of your finances; you can see pretty clearly how much comes in and how much goes out.

The first and most obvious sign of trouble is when more money goes out than what comes in. Beyond that, even if more money comes in than goes out, the question is: to what degree and in what direction. One of your goals should be to maximize your contributions to all forms of savings. Another goal should be to minimize debt of any kind. This can be accomplished by spending less in other areas; this of course, is the hard part.

This is a good time to take a break and turn your attention away from the "storyboard", and turn toward some serious thoughts about your goals in life (mutual goals if you have a life partner). You may want to refer back to the chapter on Goals in this book. Once you think you have a handle on your goals, return to the "storyboard" and honestly assess whether or not your current situation will lead you to success in obtaining those goals, and approximately when that success is likely to be reached, if at all. If you cannot figure this out easily, or you are confused, you need help from a professional or trusted person you know who has been successful in these matters.

I will assume that you can handle this process on your own; I believe you can do this if you really want to. So, let's assume that the conclusion you arrive at is that you are not currently, nor are you likely in the near future, to be on a track that leads to fulfillment of your financial goals. In fact, let's assume that you are actually moving in an opposite direction; you are either barely keeping your head above water or you are sinking deeper into debt.

Now let's go back to the "storyboard" and make decisions about where to begin to make substantive changes, based on your goals. As I said before, one of your goals should be to contribute to savings (or more into savings). How, when, and where you make cuts or changes will depend on the severity of your debt or problems. Nothing should be considered sacred or untouchable. Begin with things that are not considered bare necessities; be brutally honest here. For example, daily coffee at Starbucks, going out to eat, CDs and DVDs, magazine subscriptions, $100 sneakers, $80 jeans, $70 sunglasses, golf every weekend, weekly manicures, cell phones, mall-shopping for entertainment, etc. These are just a few of life's unnecessary items. This applies whether or not you are too much in debt. I think you get the idea here; I can't possibly cover all the non-vital things we spend money on.

Depending on your particular situation, the severity of your debt, the amount of stress you experience, the degree to which it causes discord and/or hardship in your relationship with your partner, and the real potential for any expected rapid increase in income. You may have to consider some of the following actions, barring a sudden inheritance. Buy or rent a smaller and less expensive house than the one you are currently living in. Own or buy-to-own a less expensive automobile (it really is just transportation); sell vacation homes, adult toys such as RVs, boats, motorcycles, etc. Make substantive lifestyle changes until such time as you get your financial house in order, and can get into the habit of being real honest about money. So many of the "things" we do and that we possess should not have a place in our lives until we have our lives in place.

Now that you have dissected the information on your "storyboard", you must decide, in a balanced and personal manner, to make cuts and changes in your lifestyle and spending habits. When you have done that, then it is time to commit to making that your new standard of living. You may need to express daily positive affirmations to yourself about the importance of what you are doing. This process will probably be difficult for many of you; but the outcome will be well worth your efforts to implement these positive and reparative changes in your personal financial behavior. You must believe in yourself, the process, and the direction you are going, in order for this change to work.

Relative to the severity of your situation, it may take months or years to get your financial house in order; but you absolutely must do whatever it takes to accomplish this life- changing remodel. There is a lot of trial-and-error, and there are likely to be setbacks throughout this process. Please stick with it and be patient with the process and with yourself.

Remember that money really should not be about the moment as much as it should be about tomorrow. If we work on being real honest about what we need, we will be able to fulfill, in time, some of our wants. I cannot overemphasize the importance of self-protection in preparation for unforeseen future problems that can devastate you and your family. Commit to getting informed and educated about ways to change destructive financial behavior. If you need a mathematical illustration of the budgeting process, please see the chapter entitled "Do The Math", in this book.

Support

We all need a social support system around us and as part of our lives. Support can come from a spouse, parent, relative, family friend, work associate, or social friend; or all of the above. Find at least one person who wants to be supportive of your efforts to change your personal financial behavior; in most cases this will be your spouse or life partner. Don't be ashamed or afraid to be honest with this significant-other in your life, regarding the changes you may have to make in your lifestyle and spending habits.

Also, don't be surprised if some of your so-called friends don't act so friendly anymore, once you make changes and start spending less, and doing less for entertainment. Your real friends will adjust and stick by you; the others don't matter. What matters most is getting out of trouble and out of the habit of making poor choices. You are the same (or should be) person whether you make and spend $30,000 a year, $70,000 a year, or $200,000 a year. Family and real friends should be there for one another in times of need; accept the support, be thankful for it, and reciprocate when it is your turn to be supportive of others.

Do the Math

If you are struggling with the mechanics of budgeting, and you would like detailed examples of both a problematic budget and a more successful version, perhaps the following will help you in a more graphic manner. I will present you with a real situation. I will call this person John. You will see two Tables of budgets; Table A, which is the approximate real budget of this person, and Table B, which is the budget this person might have chosen in order to be more successful at achieving some goals and accumulating savings.

John is a 31 year old single man living in a rented house with roommates. John is self- employed and has an annual gross income of approximately $60,000; his net income after taxes is approximately $45,000. At the end of every year in the recent past, John has struggled financially and has had to borrow money in order to pay year-end taxes; he has no savings or emergency funds. Why is John struggling, you might ask? Because he can't say "no" to his impulses; his drive for gratification is stronger than his drive to plan for the future; John lacks self-discipline when it comes to money. You might be thinking that a single person making this much money would not be in this kind of a predicament. It really doesn't matter how much you make if you end-up spending whatever you take in, at whatever your income level happens to be.

Let's get back to John. The total rent for the house John lives in is modest for the area; John's portion is one-third. He could budget the full amount of the rent and in so-doing, be putting an amount equal to two-thirds into a savings account. John has a vehicle that was pretty expensive to buy new; and he has been paying fairly high interest on a long term loan. It also happens to be a gas guzzler. John loves to travel and have adventures, so he takes long and expensive vacations to far-off destinations. Consequently, he not only spends quite a bit on the vacations themselves, he suffers a loss of income for the period of time he is gone; that creates a double whammy. For example, if John also loses another $4,000 to $5,000 by not working during that period of time. So the vacation ends up costing between $8,000 and $9,000.

John also has expensive hobbies and adult toys: a boat, motorcycles, snow mobile, snow- boards, hunting and fishing gear, etc. Like most of us who are fortunate and able, John does have to spend money on health insurance and other important kinds of insurance. But it really isn't the necessities that get him in to trouble and in a bind for cash, it is the money spent on WANTS rather than NEEDS that is the problem.

So, how could John have been doing things differently in order not to have the money problems he has been experiencing? First, when John started working full-time, and had a good steady income, he should have established some goals and created a budget commensurate with those goals (we will assume he did not do this). When he decided to buy a new vehicle, he should have purchased a smaller or less expensive car (new) with one of those 0% interest loans. He definitely should not have bought a boat or any other large-expenditure toys. He also should not have taken any vacations until he had saved an amount of money equal to, or greater than at least six months of income. Although this advice applies to everyone, it is most important for anyone who is self-employed. The purpose is to have a cushion in the event of unforeseen layoffs, injuries, illness, or business-related capital expenditure.

Once this six month-fund has been saved, perhaps he could buy a toy or take a short, inexpensive vacation. I recommend that only one large toy be purchased in any given year or two, so that the owner has ample time to see what it really costs to buy, own, and maintain the toy; and what kind of supplemental expenses might go along with the toy and it's lifestyle. Vacations are great and necessary but you must save for them, always making sure that you are not robbing from one budget item to feed another.

Let's take a look at some real numbers in a "Before" and "Instead" approach to John's situation:

DENNIS PEZZATO, PHD.

Table A — Before

Projected Income: $60,000

Actual Income: 55,000
(lost time for vacation)

Expenses:
Taxes 14,000
Insurances 7,000
Rent & Util. 7,000
Vehicle Payment 7,000
Vehicle Maint/gas 3,000
Toys Misc. 5,000
Business 3,000
Food/Entertain 5,000
Vacations 4,000
Coffee/lunches 2,000

Total Expenses:: $57,000

No savings — In the hole 2,000

Table B — Instead

Projected Income: $60,000
Expenses:
Taxes 15,000
Insurances 6,000
Rent & Util. 7,000
Vehicle Payment 4,000
Vehicle Maint/gas 2,000
Toys Misc. 0
Business 3,000
Food/Entertain 3,000
Vacations 0
Coffee/lunches 1,000

Total Expenses:: $41,000

Savings of $19,000

Grab Bag Items

"The more you make, the more you spend." This was a quote from my father, Joe Pezzato (now 85 years of age). I can remember hearing him say that most of my life. I didn't really understand the full meaning of those words until I was almost 30 years of age. There is nothing wrong with spending more and raising your standard of living as your earnings increase; the problems arise when you spend all of your money without putting a portion aside for savings, or when you spend more than you actually bring in.

While in pursuit of the things we WANT, we frequently miss out on the things we NEED.

"Living for today" and "living for the moment" are nice sentiments and attitudes when we're talking about getting in touch with oneself and enjoying our individual journeys through life, but those same sentiments and attitudes when applied to personal financial behavior can lead to many problems. Planning financial strategies and sound saving and spending habits are a necessary part of responsible living. The quality and security of our tomorrows depend on what we do today with an eye on tomorrow. We could all benefit from spending more time being positive about what we have, instead of being negative about what we don't have.

Conclusion and Overview

I want to do everything I can to help others prevent and minimize unnecessary struggles wherever possible. I also want to help others understand themselves in ways that will help in the development of new attitudes about themselves and others; develop new coping skills; and build a greater sense of how to discern and direct personal behavior in a manner that will be most productive and responsible.

Life presents us with endless opportunities and challenges, and sometimes the process of living can be overwhelming. One of the keys for us, especially as adults, is to try to keep our lives as simple, organized, and full of giving as possible. Another key is to try to recognize and control personal behavior that can lead to destructive, rather than constructive consequences. This requires us to be constantly aware of what we're doing; it requires us to monitor and assess the outcomes of our actions.

When it comes to your personal financial behavior, it is critical that you keep these things in mind. With education, hard work, reasonable expectations, patience, a positive attitude, and a spirit of caring and giving, you can accomplish anything in life. Successful attainment of personal goals, especially money matters, is all about you and your personal behavior and choices.

Suggested Reading List

*Anything written by Suzie Orman

*Anything written by Dave Ramsey

Success through A Positive Mental Attitude
by Napoleon Hill and W. Clement Stone

Looking Out for #1 by Robert J. Ringer
Million Dollar Habits by Robert J. Ringer

Marriage Doesn't Come With Instructions:

A Pocket Guide To Planning a Life Together

Dennis Pezzato, Ph.D.

Buonsenso Press
Cambria, California

Contents

Preface

You should wake up each day and ask yourself what you can do to make your marriage better. There is no road map available to guide couples through the process of learning how to prepare for and adjust to being married. Nor are there foolproof instructions for developing a healthy, satisfying lifelong relationship. Are you prepared for the new changes and commitments you are about to experience? The aim of this book is to give you some ideas to consider while contemplating your life with that other special person.

If you love and respect your mate enough to allow him or her to be the individual to whom you were attracted, and if you embrace his or her differences then you will be practicing the formula for a successful marriage.

Introduction

My purpose in writing this book is to share with you my opinions and ideas about how to prepare for marriage in a way that will promote a healthy, loving, respectful, and lasting relationship. Accomplishing a successful relationship can be a difficult and often frustrating process. For the most part, none of us were given any formal training in marital relations, so we used our parents' marriage as well as the marriages of other family members as examples, some good, some not so good. For the most part we are left to fly by the seat of our pants and struggle through the process. Struggle is certain to be part of marriage, but to be healthy it should be open to balance — a two-way street. I've found that if you can develop an understanding of some basic principles of human behavior and relationships that will help you to organize your thoughts and opinions, then you can put together a kind of a road map — through marriage. Along the way there will be signs to watch for that warn about bumps, stops, detours, slow going, caution, dangerous intersections, and dead ends which you'll want to avoid. If you create such a road map, it will help you be more realistic and understanding about the inevitable changes in marriage both you and your mate will experience.

How to Utilize this Book

This is not intended to be a how-to book or an all-inclusive text. I pose questions and share opinions and concepts for you to consider. I suggest that you evaluate the validity of what is stated and formulate your own view. If you find an idea in this book that has merit for you, I suggest you have conversations with your future spouse or partner and discuss how you might implement the idea.

After reading this book I encourage you to follow-up by reading other books by experts in the field of marital relations and other material on adult relationships. Get educated in every way you can so that you can attain a clearer understanding of the relational processes which lie ahead for both of you. Also, when you've finished with this book, please see my suggested reading list at the back of the book. I believe the books on this list will benefit you in ways that may increase your understanding of human dynamics in a marriage.

Human Relationships

It is my belief that relationships in life hold the keys to much, if not all of our personal happiness and mental health. We owe it to ourselves and others to strive for the most healthy, positive, loving, sharing, and caring relationship possible with our spouses, family, friends, and those with whom we share our life experiences.

We can choose to be givers who demonstrate our caring feelings through behavior and actions, or we can choose to be takers who are willing to receive demonstrations of love and caring from others without reciprocating feeling of our own. A valuable relationship is based on mutual effort and understanding.

The more you understand the motivation for the acts of the other person the easier it will be for the two of you to coexist. The more understood a person feels by another, the easier it will be to make adjustments, changes, and concessions to create a more mutually satisfying and harmonious relationship.

How Different Are We?

Aside from the obvious differences in physical make-up externally and internally, men and women are genetically and temperamentally programmed quite differently.

Generally speaking, women, by virtue of their reproductive natures, tend to be the nesters who have a need for stability, security, and have an inborn capacity for nurturance. Women are somewhat more inclined than men toward sensitivity and the creation of deep connections with others, as well as establishing close relationships.

Men tend to be less emotionally invested in the home or nest. Quite often their relationships are based less on emotional fellowship and more on casual camaraderie. Men are not typically as good at listening as women. Men are more power and conquest oriented than women.

Female hormonal patterns are more complex and varied than males. The brute strength of men is fifty percent stronger than women. Heart rates differ; blood pressures differ. We are just different! Learn to accept and embrace the differences! Along with this recognition there needs to be a concerted effort toward a greater understanding of real differences. We must learn to adjust to those differences.

Self Connection

Before you think seriously about sharing the rest of your life with someone with whom you are going to spend so much time, energy, and emotion, get to know yourself. Try to understand as best you can what your strengths and weaknesses are and generally what kind of a person you see yourself as being. Write down your self-appraisal.

Once you've accomplished this and it is time to get serious about a long term relationship, share yourself with that special person by revealing this most personal information. It is extremely important for both of you to share and expose your inner selves. Share fears, joys, tears, dreams, and laughter. You'll be freer together for it.

Self Disclosure

Before the marriage, try to have discussions with your partner during which each of you share at least one personal fear, hope, or dream. I'm not talking about a house, or a new car you may want to buy. I am referring to the exploration of deep personal feelings you don't necessarily share with others. These moments of sharing deep feelings and emotions will allow you both to gain more knowledge, understanding, and insights into the essence of the real person with whom you plan to share your life.

The more we understand how each of us thinks, feels, and functions, the more likely we will be able to mesh as a couple. The more intimately we are connected, the deeper and better- grounded our relationships will be.

Plan the Marriage
Before the Wedding

It seems that more often than not, couples spend countless hours of their valuable time planning every last detail of the pre-wedding, wedding, and post-wedding ceremonies and celebrations. They and their families want everything to be perfect. This scenario seems to be quite common and traditional. By comparison, I wonder how many of these couples spend at least an equal amount of time, energy, and emotions on planning the important details of the marriage — their lives together. It is almost as though we think the marriage will automatically work out; or we'll just deal with things as they pop up.

Well, let me burst your bubble with a dose of reality. That approach is not likely to work very well. Just as your wedding (which is one day out of your lives) requires effort and planning in order to turn out the way you would like, so also does the rest of your married lives together — considerably longer — require effort and planning.

Whose Wedding Is It?

Though you may not have thought about it, there may be unexpected pressures placed on you by your parents and family, and by your fiancé's parents and family. It is respectful and responsible to listen and consider the parental feelings and requests. But, only to the degree that you sincerely agree or wish to accede to their wishes. However, for the most part you should plan for, and do, what pleases you. Besides, it is almost impossible to make everyone happy; so focus primarily on you and your future spouse, with patience and consideration for others.

And, oh yes, don't forget to establish a REASONABLE and AFFORDABLE budget, especially if you and your betrothed are footing the bill. Do not put yourselves in the position of having to sacrifice financially for years to come, just for the sake of going overboard on a thirty minute ceremony and a one-day event. Think about all the days that will follow. Don't start off your marriage deep in debt. Start your marriage by learning the most valuable lesson of your financial lives together — learn to live according to your means. If you have to go into debt, you probably can't afford it.

This Is a Partnership

Fifty-fifty sounds reasonable in many ways, but I believe that each partner must be willing to give 100% all of the time. A marital partnership requires 100% commitment and constant effort in order to not only sustain itself, but to grow and flourish. The definition of Partnership means there is, or should be, an equalness and a fair togetherness. This attitude is healthy and necessary to prevent one or the other partner from feeling slighted or less important than the other. This does not mean that partners do not assume more or less importance in different roles and express different degrees of influence at times. Rather, partner equality means that each partner is one half of an undivided whole and of equal importance in the life they share together as well as in relational decisions. Individual decisions which are being made should always give consideration to the wishes, feelings, and sensitivities of both partners.

A Family Matter

Family really does matter. Each person's family of origin played an important, if not critical role in that individual's development and personality. One's family can certainly have an impact on various aspects of one's future. In the case of marriage, it is a future that includes a spouse or life partner. Not only do our families of origin in part define who we are, the parental family of both partners will continue to influence various aspects of the marital relationship.

Families are extremely important, and are often influential. Sometimes our individual immediate family members put direct or indirect pressure on the relationship decisions of the two marrieds with specific expectations. A healthy, loving, sharing, respectful, and reciprocal family relationship is what the new couple should strive for and cherish. However, the married couple should put each partner and the marriage first in all things. Next to yourself, your partner must be the most important person in your life. Give due respect and consideration to parental family, pressures, but put each other first.

Money Matters

Don't waste time or stick your head(s) in the sand about this issue. Get down to bare- bones philosophies regarding earning, saving, and spending. Although circumstances can and do change over time, be real honest with each other about all financial matters. Communicate to your partner your individual as well as combined short, medium, and long-term goals. If you cannot identify specific goals, then it is time to get some.

You need a plan for now and a plan for later. You must be open and honest with yourselves about NEEDS versus WANTS. Disagreements over money management is one of the most fought-over issues in a marriage, and can cause insurmountable differences between partners unless there is honesty, compatibility, flexibility, and compromise.

Divorce,
No Longer a Dirty Word

With more than half of marriages in the U.S. ending in divorce these days, it seems that we define the word commitment somewhat loosely. Are half of us not really serious about staying together? Are half of us bad or unlucky at choosing a mate? Are some of us too selfish to share our lives with another person — really share?

Perhaps many of us are a little self- absorbed and too inflexible to understand what it really takes to commit to another person with whom, supposedly, we are in love enough to make a commitment for a lifetime. Perhaps we just don't have the tools to understand how marriage is supposed to work. Or perhaps we just don't take the time to get to know the other person well, and then formulate a plan that will serve as a foundation for a permanent relationship.

This is worth repeating: More than one half of all marriages are ending in divorce. I realize I may not be talking about you, but I may be talking to the person next to you. I'd like you to think about that — real hard!

Premarital Counseling — Checklist

Premarital counseling may be a good way for couples to gain insight into each other's values, perspectives, and assumptions about each other and about a future together. Seeing a minister, a marriage counselor, or other mental health care professional would be well worth your time. If that is something you don't see as beneficial, then at least make up your own list of issues and questions you think should be important to consider as part of your own premarital self-counseling. Following are some examples of issues you may feel are important:

- Where will we live?
- Will we both work full time?
- Will we have children? When? How many?
- Will one of us be a stay-at-home parent?
- How do we plan on raising our kids? (See: ordering instructions in the back of this book for: *Kids Don't Come With Instructions.*)
- Are there religious differences?
- Do we have short, medium, or long-term goals?
- Can we define our goals?
- Can we define our roles?
- What about in-laws and family?
- Who handles the finances?
- Do we agree on spending, saving, and retirement?
- Is sex before marriage an issue?
- Do we have any doubts or concerns about each other?
- Do we have role expectations about each other?

You can't plan for everything but you should spend time answering as many questions as you can. Your answers will help you discover responses from your intended or yourself that require exploring. Also your answers will help you both understand your partner better, and provide you with a glimpse into the possible problem areas (bumps) in the future of the relationship.

Let's Just Talk

It is no secret that women tend to talk more frequently and more openly than men. I think this reality is part biological and part sociological. Although that fact may never change to any large degree, it does not mean that some effort at compromise won't result in a more satisfying level of sharing and reciprocal communication. Men and women both have to understand that there are also some emotional differences between the sexes that will never change.

Work with what you've got, put forth patient effort, and you will be rewarded by one another. Also keep in mind that active listening is more important than speaking. I have heard it said that what a woman wants most in a man is Big Ears. She wants him to hear what she says to him.

Marital Communication

Effective communication is much more than speaking honestly, it is a skill that most of us never learn. Communication is our means of understanding one another. It means to be tuned in to the inferences spoken in the words of your companion. It means to be in vocal sympathy with one another. Another way of putting it is to be on the same page during conversations. We must learn to listen more attentively, express our wishes more effectively, and convey an attitude of cooperativeness with an open mind.

When we speak, it is important that we speak in a manner that is easily understood by the listener. It is our responsibility to make sure the listener really gets what we intended to give to him or her. The listener cannot hear our internal thoughts, only our external words.

Also, when we listen, we need to pay careful attention to the speaker's perspective. To be an effective listener you need to have a sincere interest in what the speaker has to say, otherwise you are likely only to receive part of the intended message. The most beneficial form of communication requires both participants to be active in the process with an interested and involved attitude. A positive attitude conveys respect for the other person.

More on Communication

Differing assumptions can cause misunderstandings and arguments —
a failure to communicate. An accurate understanding of assumptions is a
critical prerequisite to effective communication. It is important to establish the foundation of understanding so your listener knows your perspective and communication intent. If you have trouble communicating, try
writing a letter (when you are calm), make an appointment to talk in a
neutral location, or draw a picture or series of pictures that tell the story of
how you feel. If all of these things fail then seek professional help.

Don't be Afraid
to Question Yourself

As part of the normal course of living, we are constantly having thoughts and feelings. When we interact with another person, we often have what are called automatic thoughts which are quick and fleeting reactions to words or gestures coming from another person. We do not take the time to really understand the intended meanings behind the words we react to. Consequently we frequently trigger negative emotions in ourselves and create unpleasant feelings between one another. When a negative automatic thought occurs, it would be beneficial for you to question your interpretation and response in order to clarify the person's intent.

Gratification

A hallmark characteristic of the generation of young adults born since approximately 1970-1980 is instant gratification. Prior to this period, and going back in time in our culture, delayed gratification was the norm. Most of today's grandparents and great-grandparents expected to work hard, plan and save for what they wanted in life. They had been taught and were willing to wait. The modern approach is to want it all and want it all now, or as soon as possible. This attitude is weighted with delusions, the failure to grasp reality, disappointment, and real trouble.

What does all of this have to do with marriage? The mindset that is driven by the need for instant gratification works against longevity in the marriage. Our expectations may be unrealistic regarding what and how soon we can attain marital happiness once infatuation passes, and reality sets in. It isn't reasonable to expect the relationship between two opposites to be perfect at the start. Humans are complicated. Instant marital bliss just won't happen. The more realistic your expectations, the more likely the marriage will endure. It takes time and effort to build marital happiness and fulfillment. Patience and hard work are usually rewarded in life!

Physical Attraction

It is reasonable to make the assumption that you are physically attracted to your future spouse. If you were not drawn to her or his physicality, would he or she be someone you would enjoy as a friend? If your answer is no, there is probably little chance for that relationship to succeed. Hormones may help get us together but they are not likely to keep us together. Physical attraction is a realistic and normal part of a male- female relationship, but it should not be the single or most predominant feature on which to base a long-term loving life together.

Once you have chosen a mate for all the right reasons, certainly you should strive for a physically healthy lifestyle that will help insure quality and longevity. Each of you will appreciate and respond to a mate who strives to retain his or her physical appeal for the other.

Romance and Sex

As I pointed out in the previous chapter, sexual love is not enough to sustain a marriage. Romance is so much more than having sex. Romantic gestures of overt affection such as kissing, stroking, touching, and hand-holding, are all elements of physical and emotional glue that keep the relationship connected in an intimate way.

Romance also strengthens the bond of marriage by liking your partner not only for her or his appealing personality, but for imperfect traits that may be endearing. Romance means the exciting and quiet moments of companionship which are enhanced by such thoughtful gestures as coming home with flowers for no special occasion; or a last minute decision to go out for a private dinner for two, snuggling by the fire for precious minutes just talking and enjoying being together.

In the real world, romance is in the eye of the beholder. It is defined on a very individual basis. It would be wise for each of us to become aware of those things which our partner feels are romantic. Enjoy the process of discovering your partner's romantic preferences and desires. And remember romance should be a reciprocal process.

Remember that the tone and intimacy of your relationship for the half hour of sexual contact is set by the strength of your relationship in the other twenty-three and a half hours of the day. In other words, the degree to which you have a harmonious and loving relationship without sex, will determine in part the degree to which you have a pleasing, romantic sexual relationship.

Temptation and Infidelity

If you don't allow yourself to be in situations in which temptations are more likely to occur, you probably won't be tempted. If you find yourself in a situation not of your own choosing, in which temptation is present, you must find a way to remove yourself. If you cannot physically turn away then you should try to change your mental perception of the object of temptation or find a way to distract yourself with other thoughts.

Regardless of the form temptation takes or the status of your relationship with your partner, you need to exert control over yourself. This is especially true if you are living in a troublesome or unsatisfying relationship. You owe it to yourself, your partner, and your children (if you have children) to do EVERYTHING possible to repair the injured relationship BEFORE you look elsewhere to find what you feel you don't have. The grass is seldom as green on the other side of the street as it appears to be when you are dissatisfied with your marriage.

What About Children?

This is a biggie. This is a topic that should be discussed in depth prior to wedding plans and prior to pregnancy. This is an individual and personal matter which requires thorough communication between partners.

Relationships such as marriage require effort and adjustment as well as some time to settle-in to experience life as the "two of us" rather than the "me" life you've left behind. The decision when or if to have children is part of the getting to know each other process. Once you both agree that you will have children, then you must decide when and how many.

Making a plan you both feel comfortable with regarding how you will raise your children will probably be the toughest of your considerations. Please believe me when I suggest that you really will benefit from having a plan, and by agreeing as much as possible on most, if not all aspects of your plan. There are many excellent books available on parenting. Naturally, I strongly recommend that you read my first book *Kids Don't Come With Instructions: A Pocket Guide To Raising Children* My book is easy to read and understand. In it you will find a suggested reading list as well. I urge you not to bring children into the world unless you both feel strongly about wanting to be parents. If you have trouble making the decision or agreeing with each other, then by all means seek counsel from parents, family, clergy, or a mental health professional.

DO NOT, I repeat, DO NOT have a child as a means to fix an ailing relationship. The odds are that the presence of a child will strain an already unstable situation, and one result could be the demise of the relationship. If two people cannot coexist in relative harmony, then certainly three or more cannot make life simpler or easier, or more harmonious. No child should have to bear the burden of fixing his or her parents' marriage or living with the result of their divorce.

DENNIS PEZZATO, PHD.

More About Children

Couples who decide to have children should make certain that their relationship is on solid ground with mutually agreed upon life- paths and family planning prior to having children. Parenting is probably the most difficult and certainly the most important job in life. You owe it to your yet-to-be-born children to be the best pre-parent couple possible. And you will owe it to your children to maintain the best married partnership your continual efforts can produce.

Feeling Deprived?

During pregnancy and after the birth of a child (especially your first child), many physiological, psychological, and emotional changes occur. It is unrealistic for either marital partner to expect life to be as it was before this period, especially the amount of attention given to each other. Children need attention and fulfilling that need subtracts from the precious moments you and your partner shared when there were just two of you. Each of us has only so much to give before exhaustion, frustration, and irritability sets in. Be as supportive of each other as possible. Extend yourself and be patient. Baby caring is a new time and a new experience for both of you. Take care of one another and try lowering your expectations of each other. Be open to the changes that will occur every single day and integrate those changes into your lives to create a new relational and family pattern.

Date Night

Date night can be a refreshing and exciting reunion of the two of you if you give some thoughtful planning for maximum romantic effect. It can become a tradition that you will look forward to if you plan it as an adventure. Date night does not have to cost a lot, and it becomes a little (or a lot) more difficult to do after you have children. Work commitments sometimes get in the way as well as any number of other "important" things you must get done. However, this is a must-do you should fit into your busy lives.

Once a week you should schedule and keep date night. This date should be for as long a period as possible, and is best done away from the home environment. Getting away from distractions and concentrating on your selves is the whole purpose. At the risk of losing some readers, I also suggest you leave all high-tech gadgets at home or work. Yes, that means cell phones too. The main exception to this would be if you absolutely are required to be available for emergencies only.

The idea here is to have some real alone time with your mate, doing something you both enjoy doing together. Couples absolutely need to cultivate and renew their intimate connections with one another. Make it a point to set aside a few hours together. You will be surprised how they will revive and expand your appreciation of those virtues in your partner that attracted you to her or him. Even a couple of hours together are beneficial. Perhaps you could go for a bike ride, a walk, a quick meal, a cup of coffee, or even a motel room. This is therapy you'll grow to count on.

Roles in Marriage

For those of you not familiar with the term role, it basically refers to an individual's function or participation which requires certain behavior. For example, traditionally, the man has performed the function or role of participating as a husband, which may entail being the chief provider of the family income. He also may function as the handyman, the cook, the bill payer, the person in charge of the automobiles and other mechanical things. Likewise the woman assumes the role of the wife, homemaker, second job holder, the children's primary caregiver, the house cleaner, the gardener, and the school liaison.

We all adopt roles in a marital relationship based on our beliefs, lessons from our families of origin, and whatever we negotiate with our mate that seems appropriate for our relationship. This can be very much a trial and error process, or it can be pre-planned prior to marriage and implemented temporarily or permanently.

There will also be times when roles may change based on altered life circumstances or changes in your personal perspectives. Make these decisions carefully and thoughtfully— together. In addition to the multitude of roles which get created, we assume the subtle roles of best friend, lover, and confidant. All of this makes for interesting and challenging participation in what should be a lifelong commitment to one another.

Is It Good for Me?

This expression reflects an attitude in many young marrieds which should be reversed. Is it good for her or him? should replace the first person emphasis if you are going to have a strong marriage. I am talking about filling the emotional needs of your partner, not just the physical requirements. No one can be all things to all people, and certainly none of us is the perfect mate. Truth be known, few of us really expect our mates to be perfect.

However, I must point out we can always try to be mindful of doing things that help fulfill the needs of our partner. Attempt to put forth the necessary effort to accommodate what's best for your partner on a regular basis, not once a year, but at least once a day if possible.

It is important to get feedback from your partner about his or her needs. Ask for specific feedback from her or him. It will provide the information you require to help you give what your partner desires. Your partner, of course, must be asked to be honest and candid. Without it you are less likely to be able to adjust your efforts appropriately.

Self-Interests

Husbands and wives need to have their own interests, hobbies, and friends who each pursues separately as individuals. There are times when we all need to participate in activities without our partners; to do something that we identify with only ourselves. We may be devoted to the "we-ness" in life, but it is healthy also to focus on the "me-ness" in life. There is no "we" without "me".

If you try to hinder your partner's times apart from you, it may have a destructive influence on the relationship. Also, dependency on your partner for everything you need is asking more than what most relationships can provide.

Your personal development is essential to the health of your marriage. It is through this developmental process that you can build and sustain self-esteem, self-worth, and expand who you are. If you value yourself, your partner will value you. If you strive to make yourself the best that you can be, it will likely lead to an enhanced marital relationship and will also motivate your partner to do the same.

Whose Goals Matter Most?

His, Hers, Theirs?

Part of the process and purpose of learning about one another is to understand what aspects of life are most important. Prior to any discussions regarding these issues, I suggest each person makes a written list itemizing, in order of importance and priority, your individual goals and marital goals as a couple.

Once you've made your list, you should compare it with your partner's in order to understand its importance to him or her. More importantly, the list proves how the two of you can achieve as many personal and mutual goals as possible. This process may take considerable time, effort, flexibility, adaptability, and compromise. You must be honest with yourself and with your partner. You both need to be able to define and separate NEEDS from WANTS, and be realistic about accomplishing both.

Who Is Number One?

He is! She is! You both should consider each other as number one in your lives, forever. Oh yes, I realize there are times when the children will seem to consume your existence, but don't let those periods prevent you from being committed to your relationship with your mate. Always find the time each day to have private time, no matter how brief that time may be. Always take the time each day to let your mate know how much you love and appreciate him or her.

Swap Roles for One Day

Whenever a person does a job or task well that job looks relatively simple and easy to the observer. This view applies to almost every job, task, skill, or talent in most normal settings. It is pretty easy to observe someone performing his or her role and to judge the degree of difficulty — or so we think. The fact is that unless we have done the same job under similar circumstances, for a similar length of time, we really do not know as much as we think we do.

It is common, natural, and unfair to presume to really know what it is like to actually walk in the shoes of another person. In an attempt not to take your spouse or partner for shadow each other for an entire day. This will enable you to gain a new perspective and a greater appreciation for the other person. If you can accomplish this, you will likely improve your relationship and have a greater respect for your mate.

Begin Each Day

Make a real effort to begin each day, no matter what, by sharing a smile, a hug, a kiss, and say something positive to your partner (when you have children, each one should be included in this ritual).

Each person should wake up and ask "what can I do "today" to make the marital relationship better. Not only is this positive behavior catching, but it is a wonderful gift to give to each other. Once you have children, there is no greater gift to give your children than to begin each day with a positive affirmation. This daily approach will contribute to parents who have a sustained loving, caring, and giving relationship.

At the End of Each Day

Every day you are together, try to end it with a smile, a hug, a kiss, a "thank-you," or an "I love you." Never go to sleep mad at one another. Try to resolve disagreements, or at least temporarily agree to disagree. Don't let the sun set on an angry environment. At the same time, remind one another of your love and commitment to each other. Endeavor to work on the resolution of a problem as soon as possible. End your day with a prayer or a positive thought about the day and your appreciation of your partner. Sleeping with a smile is so much healthier than sleeping with a frown, both physically and emotionally.

Change — Is It Good?

It may be good; it may not be so good, but change will happen. It is important to recognize and understand that when one partner changes, whether the change is positive, negative, or somewhere in between, the relationship changes. The preexisting balance will have been impacted. Any substantive change can disturb the balance. Do not deny change, but work with the changes as you adjust to the influences they bring. Communicate with your partner about any change you are experiencing. Constant change is inevitable. It requires continual adjustments in the relationship. Keep in mind that successful adjustments require ongoing communication.

Remember that no matter how much we agree on things, and how many things we share in common, we are all individuals with different beliefs based on our backgrounds. Acknowledge your partner's position or change as being different from yours, not necessarily wrong, bad, or unreasonable—just different.

See a Problem
for What It Really Is

When interacting with, and judging our spouses, we tend to attach symbolic meanings, perfectionism, and moralistic evaluations to practical everyday problems. Everyday tasks and chores should not be burdened with emotional biases. Think, for example, of the task being performed by a friend or neighbor instead of your mate. The level of evaluation and criticism should be very different if you do this. Try to be less judgmental of your mate and more accepting of his or her individualism. Don't make a mountain out of a mole hill.

Schedule Strong Disagreements

Be smart about when and where you have strong disagreements. Of course there are going to be minor disagreements that pop up and must be dealt with immediately (or so we think). I'm referring to reoccurring "hot button" issues such as money, sex, children, chores, annoying habits or personality traits. These issues can be so large and so important, that you need to discuss, debate, and negotiate them at a time when you are both calm, rested, and have time set aside to devote to resolution. This time should be viewed as an opportunity to reasonably negotiate your needs within the relationship. Be respectful of your beloved's point of view and stated needs. Try to understand his or her perspective, no matter how difficult that may be for you. If you can describe and understand your partner's point of view to his or her satisfaction, then you will have helped to establish common ground for negotiation and a basis for implementing change upon which you both can agree.

If you already have children or are planning to have children, DO NOT fight in front of them. They do not understand this process the way adults do, and they should not have to pay a price emotionally for your behavior.

Give and Take

Giving another person what she or he needs, and doing so on a frequent basis will usually mean that you will in turn, receive much of what YOU need. Most of us are reasonable and at least somewhat sensitive enough to realize when someone is sincerely trying to do things that please us. In response to that giving, we will likely give in return. "You scratch my back, and I'll scratch yours."

Emotional Bank Accounts

We all have our own private and personal emotional compartments within our minds. We can refer to them as our "emotional bank accounts". Regardless of whether we are stingy or generous givers, we all need to supplement the withdrawals from those accounts with deposits. We don't usually ask for the deposits to be made, or specify who should make them; but we definitely need them.

As a life partner, you should be making frequent and regular deposits into your loved one's emotional bank account. These deposits almost never need to be large or grand; they actually fill the account faster if they are in the form of lots of small deposits. The thoughtful words and deeds that take effort, sincerity, consideration, caring, sharing, and appreciation make up those small deposits. Emotional bank accounts which are kept full will build strength in a relationship and keep the connection strong and intimate.

How Does Your Garden Grow?

You must tend your garden daily if you expect it to flourish and be beautifully productive. You must turn the soil, pull the weeds, and provide the water in order for the sun to nourish growth, and not parch. All of these things are necessary in order not to allow your garden to gradually die off.

The natural tendency for spouses is to gradually drift apart over time unless they work at staying close and together. Working the relationship means tending the garden (each other's or the community garden). It takes a conscious, daily effort to demonstrate how much you value that which your garden produces. If you sow with grace and gratitude you will reap a life of love and devotion.

What Is It Worth?

Could you place a value on your relationship with your chosen life mate? Maybe, but I suggest you find the words to describe how valuable you feel your relationship REALLY IS. Those words should generate feelings and emotions which will reflect your motivation to make this relationship your top priority. Every day in life requires adjustments in our behavior — behavior WE choose. CHOOSE open- minded, considerate, and understanding behavior. CHOOSE to see your partner's point of view. Choose to value yourself and your partner above anything else.

Practice, Practice, Practice

What we practice most in life becomes habit to us! Both men and women need to discover the emotional needs of one another and gradually work out ways to satisfy those needs for each other. This can be very challenging at times because it may mean doing something you are not accustomed to doing. Listening not only with your ears but with your mind, your heart, and all of your senses is a challenge that requires effort, patience, and most of all, practice, practice, practice.

Grab Bag Items

In all aspects of life, and in all of your relationships, especially with your spouse, try not to react too quickly to situations that occur. Develop a personal Hold button. Put yourself on hold for a few moments and think before you react. This will allow you to consider an appropriate response rather than a hasty reaction. We tend to react before we think much more frequently than we are aware. This pause will become an enabler of control within us. Practice this technique often, it really does work.

Spend lots of time discussing the idea of living together before you decide to cohabit or get married unless you already know the details, or have already lived with your future partner. Learn what each other's preferences for lifestyle and home style are. Learn about issues such as neatness, cleanliness, organization, roles, chores, eating habits, etc. Little things about the other that irritate you or your partner can become magnified out of proportion and cause a split. It's great to love another, but if you don't like the little habits, idiosyncrasies, and personal realities of that person, they can become objectionable road bumps to a lasting relationship.

Conclusion and Overview

For the majority of us, marriage is at best a trial and error process. The time to think about marital relations is before the wedding. Try to understand that planning a life together involves looking at many different aspects of both "me" issues and "we" issues The period of courtship and infatuation are full of attraction, romance, passion, pleasing, and togetherness — all of which are warm and wonderful. But those feelings will naturally become somewhat subdued once the demands of life as a couple or a family set in. Life becomes more ordinary unless you have a plan to make it lasting and worthwhile.

Premarital exploration and planning will increase the odds of having a smoother and less stressful period of adjustment during the early years; and perhaps a more harmonious, enduring, and healthy relationship, which will endure.

Change is inevitable and growth is likely. Learn together about one another and make your marriage a priority in your lives. Educate yourselves by reading books, by talking, and by listening. Be open to counseling in the event the lines of communication become blurred or closed. Be each other's best friend, biggest fan, and most solid supporter. Always ask yourselves: Am I contributing to the relationship with my behavior or am I contaminating it with my lack of thoughtfulness? Always remember that each day is a gift; celebrate life, living, and the opportunity for giving. Give to yourselves and to others.

Suggested Reading List

Love Is Never Enough, Aaron T. Beck, M.D.

Reconcilable Differences, Andrew Christensen, Ph.D. and Neil S. Jacobson, Ph.D.

How To Live With Another Person, David Viscott, M.D.

Complete Marriage and Family Home Reference Guide, Dr. James Dobson

Renew Your Marriage at Midlife, Steve Brody and Cathy Brody

Peer Marriage: How Love Between Equals Really Works, Pepper Schwartz

Lasting marriages: Men and Women Gaining Together, Richard Mackey Bernard A. O'Brien (textbook)

Marriage Doesn't Come With Instructions:

A Pocket Guide To Sustaining A Marriage

by Dennis Pezzato, PhD.

Buonsenso Press
Cambria, California

CONTENTS

PREFACE

You should wake up each day and ask yourself what you can do to make your marriage better. There is no road map available to guide couples through the process of learning how to prepare for and sustain a marriage. Nor are there foolproof instructions for developing a healthy, satisfying, lifelong relationship. Are you comfortable in your marriage? Are you frustrated, confused, disappointed, unhappy, unfulfilled or empty?

The aim of this book is to give you some ideas to consider while contemplating your relationship in your marriage, and while contemplating your marriage as an entity to which you and your spouse or partner belong and contribute.

If you love and respect your mate enough to allow him or her to be himself or herself, and if you embrace his or her differences and celebrate his or her strengths, then you will be practicing part of a formula for a successful marriage. It is also important to understand that each of us must always be open to learning more about ourselves, one another, and our relationship.

INTRODUCTION

My purpose in writing this book is to share with you my opinions and ideas about how to improve and sustain your marriage in a way that will promote a more healthy, loving, respectful and lasting relationship. Accomplishing a successful relationship can be difficult and often frustrating process. For the most part, none of us were given any formal training in marital relations, so we used our parents' marriage, as well as the marriages of other family members as examples; some good, some not so good. We were really left to fly by the seat of our pants and struggle through the process; and struggle is certainly a part of most marriages.

In order to be healthy, a marriage should be open to balance, which is a two way street. I have found that if you can develop an understanding of some basic principles of human behavior and relationships that will help you to organize your thoughts and opinions, then you can put together a kind of road map—through marriage. Along the way there will be signs to watch for that warn about bumps, stops, detours, slow-going, caution, dangerous intersections, and dead ends, which you'll want to avoid. If you create such a road map, it will help you to be more realistic and understanding about the inevitable changes in marriage both you and your mate will experience, or indeed, have experienced already.

It is never too late to step back and take a new and fresh look at where you are now, and where you want to be.

HOW TO UTILIZE THIS BOOK

This is not intended to be a how-to book or an all-inclusive text. I pose questions and share opinions and concepts for you to consider. I suggest that you evaluate the validity of what is stated and formulate your own view. If you find an idea an in this book has merit for you, I suggest you have conversations with your spouse or partner and discuss how you might implement the idea.

After reading this book I encourage you to follow-up by reading other books by experts in the field of marital relations and other material on adult relationships. Get educated in every way you can so that you can attain a clearer understanding of the relational processes which you both experience. Also, when you've finish with this book, please see my suggested reading list at the back of the book. I believe they may benefit you in ways that may increase your understanding of human dynamics in marriage.

HUMAN RELATIONSHIPS

It is my belief that relationships in life hold the keys to much, if not all of our personal happiness and mental health. We owe it to ourselves and others to strive for the most healthy, positive, loving, sharing, and caring relationship possible with our spouses, family, friends, and those with whom we share our life experiences.

We choose to be givers who demonstrate our caring feelings through behavior and actions, or we can choose to be takers who are willing to receive demonstrations of love and caring from others without reciprocating feeling of our own. A valuable relationship is based on mutual effort and understanding.

The more you understand the motivation for the acts of the other person the easier it will be for the two of you to coexist. The more understood a person feels by the other, the easier it will be to make adjustments, changes, and concessions to create a more mutually satisfying and harmonious relationship.

HOW DIFFERENT ARE WE?

Aside from the obvious differences in physical make-up externally and internally, men and women are genetically and temperamentally programmed quite differently. Generally speaking, women, by virtue of their reproductive capacity, tend to be the nesters who have a need for stability, security, and have an inborn capacity for nurturance. Women are somewhat more inclined than men toward sensitivity and the creation of deep connections with others, as well as establishing close relationships.

Men tend to be less emotionally invested in the home or nest. Quite often their relationships are based less on emotional fellowship and more on casual camaraderie. Men are not typically as good at listening as women. Men are more power and conquest oriented than women. Female hormonal patterns are more complex and varied than males. The brute strength of men is said to be about fifty percent stronger than women. Heart rates differ; blood pressures differ. We are just different! Learn to accept and embrace the differences! Along with this recognition there needs to be a concerted effort toward a greater understanding of real differences. We must learn to adjust to those differences; this is an ongoing process.

SELF CONNECTION

As you continue sharing your life with someone with whom you have invested so much time, energy, and emotion, get to know yourself better. Try to understand as best you can what your strengths and weaknesses are, and generally what kind of person you see yourself as being. Write down your self-appraisal. Use the chapter in this book, Personal Inventory, to assist you in the self-appraisal process.

PERSONAL INVENTORY

This inventory has been devised to elicit an honest response from you about what you believe are your strengths and your weaknesses, as well as your major traits, tendencies, likes and dislikes. This may be a difficult exercise for some of you, so here are some recommendations to assist you in the process. Remember to take your time with this exercise. Quiet, alone-time is the best setting, without distractions. Be honest with your answers; the only person who will read them is you, unless you wish to share them. Write out your answers so that you will have them to refer to.

The sample personal inventory below may nudge you with ideas to create your own list. The purpose of the sample is to get you started. Do your best to answer these questions with a Yes or No (Y/N). Feel free to elaborate on any of these things once you have completed your initial inventory:

I am a nice person
I am honest
I am unselfish
I am loving
I am lovable
I am likable
I am hardworking
I am sincere
I am considerate of others
I am thoughtful
I am sensitive
I am open-minded
I am patient
I am caring
I like animals
I am environmentally responsible
I am fair
I am intelligent
I have integrity

I am tolerant
I am a good listener

All of the above would be considered strengths or desirable traits by most of us. The opposites of those things on the list would be considered weaknesses or undesirable traits, which can be improved upon when you acknowledge them. And of course, that is the purpose of a personal inventory—to describe who you believe yourself to be at a given stage in your life and determine how to improve on it, if you so choose.

The other beneficial aspect of a self-inventory resides in the value of the process itself, and the ever-changing discoveries of connecting with yourself. As an aside, this personal inventory, when completed by each member of a couple, can be used effectively as a tool in assessing compatibility.

SELF DISCLOSURE

As a follow-up to Self Connection, try to have discussions with your partner; during which you each share at least one personal fear, hope, or dream, preferably more than one. I'm not talking about a house or a new car you may want to buy. I am referring to the exploration of deep personal feelings you don't necessarily share with others. These moments of sharing deep feelings and emotion will allow you both to gain more knowledge, understanding, and insights into the essence of the real person with whom you share your life.

The more we understand how each of us thinks, feels, and functions, the more likely we will be able to mesh as a couple. The more intimately we are connected, the deeper and better grounded our relationships will be.

THIS IS A PARTNERSHIP

Fifty-fifty sounds reasonable in many ways but I believe that each partner must be willing to give 100% all the time. A marital partnership requires 100% commitment and constant effort in order to not only sustain itself, but to grow and flourish. The definition of Partnership means there is, or should be, an equalness and a fair togetherness. This attitude is healthy and necessary to prevent one or the other partner from feeling slighted or less important than the other. This does not mean that partners do not assume more or less importance in different roles and express different degrees of influence at times. Rather, partner equality means that each partner is one half of an undivided whole and of equal importance in life together as well as in relational decisions. Individual decisions which are being made should always give consideration to the wishes, feelings, and sensitivities of both partners.

A FAMILY MATTER

Family really does matter. Each person's family of origin played an important, if not critical role in that person's development and personality. One's family can certainly have an impact on various aspects of one's future. In the case of marriage, it is a future that includes a spouse or life partner. Not only do our families of origin in part define who we are, the parental family of both partners will continue to influence various aspects of the marital relationship.

Families are extremely important, and are often influential. Sometimes our individual immediate family members put direct or indirect pressure on the relationship decisions of the couple with specific expectations. A healthy, loving, respectful, and reciprocal family relationship is what we should all strive for and cherish. However, the married couple should put each partner and the marriage first in all things. Next to yourself, your partner must be the most important person in your life. Give due respect and consideration to parental family issues, but put each other first.

MONEY MATTERS

Don't waste time or stick your head(s) in the sand about this issue. Get down to bare-bones philosophies regarding earning, saving, and spending. Although circumstances can and do change over time, be real honest with each other about all financial matters. Communicate to your partner your individual as well as combined short, medium, and long-term goals. If you cannot identify specific goals, then it is time to get some. You need a plan for now and a plan for later. You must be open and honest with yourselves about NEEDS versus WANTS. Disagreements over money management is one of the most fought-over issues in a marriage, and can cause insurmountable differences between partners unless there is honesty, compatibility, flexibility, and compromise.

If you have children it is even more important for you to get your financial house in order. Number one, you don't want to cheat your children out of necessities in life; and number two, you absolutely do not want to teach them irresponsible money habits.

DIVORCE, NO LONGER A DIRTY WORD

With more than half of marriages in the U.S. ending in divorce these days, it seems that we define the word commitment somewhat loosely. Are half of us not really serious about staying together? Are half of us bad or unlucky at choosing a mate? Are some of us too selfish to share our lives with another person—really share?

Perhaps many of us are a little self-absorbed and too inflexible to understand what it really takes to commit to another person who we supposedly love; a commitment for a lifetime. Perhaps we just don't have the tools to understand how marriage is supposed to work. Or perhaps we just don't take the time to get to know the other person well, and then formulate a plan that will serve as a foundation for a permanent relationship. This is worth repeating: More than one half of all marriages are ending in divorce. I realize I may not be talking to you, but I may be talking to the person next to you. I'd like you to think about that—real hard!

No matter what problems or issues exist in your marriage, you owe it to yourself and to one another to exhaust every possible means of resolving differences before there is any serious consideration of divorce. If you have children, this recommendation comes with even more passion and conviction. You have no right to put your children through unnecessary turmoil and emotional instability. Relationships require constant effort and attention; and as far as I am concerned, divorce should be a dirty word and used as a last resort. Divorce usually creates more problems than it solves, especially if there are children involved.

MARITAL SELF COUNSELING—
A CHECKLIST

Marital self counseling may be a good way for couples to gain insight into each others values, perspectives, and assumptions about each other and about your lives together. Seeing a minister, a marriage counselor, or other mental health care professional would be well worth your time. If that is something you don't see as beneficial, then at least make up your own list of issues and questions you think should be important to consider as part of your own marital self counseling. Following are some examples of issues you may feel are important:

Are we in agreement about where we live?

Are we in agreement about our work careers?

Will we have children? When? How many?

Do we agree on methods of raising children?

Will one of us be a stay-at-home parent?

How do we plan on raising our children?
    (see ordering instructions in the back of this book for: *Kids Don't Come With Instructions*)

Are there religious differences?

Do we have short, medium, or long-term goals?

Can we define our goals?

Can we define our roles?

Do we have role expectations about each other that are problematic or un-communicated?

What about in-laws and family?

Who handles the finances? Do we share the responsibilities?

Do we agree on spending, saving, and retirement?

Is sex an issue?

Do we have any doubts or concerns about each other?

Are we, as individuals, content, happy, and fulfilled?

Is the status of our marriage pleasing to us?

You should spend time answering as many questions as you can. Your answers will help you elicit responses from your partner that may motivate you to explore further. The answers to your questions will help you to both understand your partner more as well as provide you with a view into the possible problem areas (bumps) in the relationship.

LET'S JUST TALK

It is no secret that women tend to talk more frequently and more openly than men. I think this reality is part biological and part sociological. Although that fact may never change to any large degree, it does not mean that some effort at compromise won't result in a more satisfying level of sharing and reciprocal communication. Men and women both have to understand that there are also some emotional differences between the sexes that will never change.

Work with what you've got, put forth patient effort, and you will be rewarded by one another. Also keep in mind that active listening is more important than speaking. I have heard it said that what a woman needs most from a man is Big Ears (ears with a heart). She wants him to hear what she says to him.

One expert I have read suggested that a really good listener should see himself or herself as a heart with ears. Couples should talk often with attention, respect, and understanding.

MARITAL COMMUNICATION

Effective communication is much more than speaking honestly, it is a skill that most of us never learn. Communication is our means of understanding one another. It means to be tuned in to the inferences spoken in the words of your companion. It means to be in vocal sympathy with one another. Another way of putting it is to be on the same page during conversations. We must learn to listen more attentively, express our wishes more effectively, and convey an attitude of cooperativeness with an open mind.

When we speak, it is important that we speak in a manner that is easily understood by the listener. It is our responsibility to make sure the listener really gets what we intended to give. The listener cannot hear our internal thoughts, only our external words. Also, when we listen, we need to pay careful attention to the speaker's perspective. To be an effective listener you need to have a sincere interest in what the speaker has to say, otherwise you are likely only to receive part of the intended message.

The most beneficial form of communication requires both participants to be active in the process with an interested and involved attitude. A positive attitude conveys respect for the other person.

Differing assumptions can cause misunderstandings and arguments—a failure to communicate. It is important to establish a foundation of understanding so your listener knows your perspective and intention. If you have trouble communicating, try writing a letter (when you are calm), make an appointment to talk in a neutral location, or draw a picture or series of pictures that tell the story of how you feel. If all of these things fail, then seek professional help.

DON'T BE AFRAID
TO QUESTION YOURSELF

As part of the normal course of living, we are constantly having thoughts and feelings. When we interact with another person, we often have what are called automatic thoughts, which are quick and fleeting reactions to words or gestures coming from another person. We do not take the time to really understand the intended meanings behind the words we react to. Consequently we frequently trigger negative emotions in ourselves and create unpleasant feelings between one another. When a negative automatic thought occurs, it would be beneficial for you to question your interpretation and response in order to clarify the intent of the person to whose words you have overreacted.

This may not be an issue for you at all, however it does seem to occur with many of us. If it does, and if you plan to do some work in this area, I suggest you start out by writing down on paper those negative automatic thoughts. This process may help you to not only have a clearer understanding of what the other person intended, but may also help you see yourself and your thoughts in a different light.

GRATIFICATION

A hallmark characteristic of the generations of young adults born since approximately 1970-1980 is instant gratification. Prior to this period, and going back in time in our culture, delayed gratification was the norm. Most of today's grandparents and great-grandparents expected to work hard, plan, and save for what they wanted in life. They had been taught and were willing to wait. The modern approach is to want it all and want it all now, or as soon as possible, regardless the cost or consequences. This attitude is weighted with delusions, the failure to grasp reality, disappointment, and real trouble.

What does all of this have to do with marriage? The mindset that is driven by the need for instant gratification works against longevity in the marriage. Our expectations may be unrealistic regarding what and how soon we can attain marital happiness once infatuation passes, and reality sets in. It isn't reasonable to expect the relationship between two opposites to be perfect at the start. Humans are complicated. Instant marital bliss just won't happen. The more realistic your expectations, the more likely the marriage will endure. It takes time and effort to build marital happiness and fulfillment. Patience and hard work are usually rewarded in life!

ROMANCE AND SEX

Sexual love is not enough to sustain a marriage. Romance is so much more than having sex. Romantic gestures of overt affection such as kissing, hugging, stroking, touching, and hand-holding are all elements of physical and emotional glue that keep the relationship connected in an intimate way.

Romance also strengthens the bond of marriage through liking your partner, enjoying the exciting and quiet moments of companionship with thoughtful gestures such as coming home with flowers for no special occasion; a last minute decision to go out for a private meal for two; snuggling by the fire (or video of a fire) or on the sofa just talking, enjoying being together. In the real world, romance is in the eye of the beholder. By this I mean that it is defined on an individual basis. It would be wise for each of us to become aware of those things that our partner feels are romantic. Enjoy the process of discovering your partner's romantic preferences and desires. And remember that romance should be a reciprocal process just as all other expressions of love.

Remember that the tone and intimacy of your relationship for the half hour of sexual contact is set by the strength of your relationship in the other twenty-three and a half hours of the day. In other words, the degree to which you have a harmonious relationship without sex, will determine in part the degree to which you have a pleasing, romantic sexual relationship.

TEMPTATION AND INFIDELITY

If you don't allow yourself to be in situations in which temptations are more likely to occur, you probably won't be tempted. If you find yourself in a situation not of your own choosing, in which temptation is present, you must find a way to remove yourself. If you cannot physically turn away then you should try to change your mental perception of the object of temptation or find a way to distract yourself with other thoughts.

Regardless of the form temptation takes or the status of your relationship with your partner, you need to exert control over yourself. This is especially true if you are living in a troublesome or unsatisfying relationship. You owe it to yourself, your partner, and your children (if you have children) to do EVERYTHING possible to repair the injured relationship BEFORE you look elsewhere to find what you feel you don't have. The grass is seldom as green on the other side of the street as it appears to be when you are dissatisfied with your marriage.

And as I frequently point out in this book, think about what harm and turmoil you may bring into the lives of your children, when you make choices that can impact their lives.

WHAT ABOUT THE CHILDREN?

This is an individual and personal matter which requires thorough communication between partners. Relationships such as marriage require effort and adjustment, as does the job of being parents. Making a plan you both feel comfortable with regarding how you will raise your children will probably be the toughest of your considerations. Please believe me when I stress that that you really will benefit from having a plan, and by agreeing as much as possible on most, if not all aspects of your plan. There are many excellent books available on parenting. Naturally, I strongly recommend that you read my first book, "Kids Don't Come With Instructions: A Pocket Guide To Raising Children". My book is easy to read and understand. In it you will find a suggested reading list as well.

I urge you not to bring children into the world unless you both feel strongly about wanting to be parents. If you have trouble making the decision or agreeing with each other, then by all means seek counsel from parents, family, clergy, or a mental health care professional. DO NOT, I repeat, DO NOT have a child as a means to fix an ailing relationship. The odds are that the presence of a child will strain an already unstable situation, and one result could be the demise of the relationship. If two people cannot coexist in relative harmony, then certainly three or more cannot make life simpler or easier, or more harmonious. No child should have to bear the burden of fixing his or her parents' marriage, or of living with the result of their divorce.

Couples who decide to have children should make certain that their relationship is on solid ground with mutually agreed upon life-paths and family planning prior to having children. Parenting is probably the most difficult and certainly the most important job in life. You owe it to your children to be the best couple possible; and you owe it to your children to maintain the best possible married partnership your continual efforts can produce.

FEELING DEPRIVED?

During pregnancy and after the birth of a child (especially your first), many physiological, psychological, and emotional changes occur. It is unrealistic for either marital partner to expect life to be as it was before this period, especially the amount of attention given to each other. Children need attention, and fulfilling that need subtracts from the precious moments you and your shared when there were just the two of you. Each of us only has so much to give before exhaustion, frustration, and irritability sets in. Be as supportive of each other as possible. Extend yourself and be patient. Baby-caring is a new time and a new experience for both of you. Take care of one another and try lowering your expectations of each other. Be open to the changes that will occur every single day and integrate those changes into your lives to create a new relational and family pattern.

Regardless of how many children you have or what their ages, mom and dad need to work at nurturing their own relationship. You each need to make one another the most important person in your lives next to yourself. Someday the children will leave the nest, and it will just be the two of you once again. Make certain your empty nest is occupied by two people who still know each other and still have some of that original excitement, passion, companionship, and love.

DATE NIGHT

Date Night is a necessity for all couples, especially those with children. Date Night can be a refreshing and exciting reunion of the two of you if you give some thought to planning for maximum romantic effect. It can become a tradition that you will look forward to if you plan it as an adventure. Date Night does not have to cost a lot, and it becomes a little (or a lot) more difficult to do after you have children. Work commitments sometimes get in the way as well as any number of other "important things" you must get done. However, this is a must-do that you should fit into your busy lives.

Once a week you should schedule and keep Date Night. This date should be for as long of a period as possible, and is best away from the home environment; getting away from distractions and concentrating on yourselves is the whole purpose. At the risk of losing some readers, I suggest you leave all high-tech gadgets at home or at work; yes, that means cell phones too. The main exception to this would be if you absolutely are required to be available for emergencies only.

The idea here is to have some real alone time with your mate, doing something you both enjoy doing together. Couples absolutely need to cultivate and renew their intimate connections with one another. Make it a point to set aside a few hours together. You will be surprised how they will revive and expand your appreciation of those virtues in your partner that attracted you to her or him. Even a couple of hours together are beneficial. Perhaps you could go for a walk, a bike ride, a quick meal, a cup of coffee, or even a motel room. This is therapy you will grow to count on.

ROLES IN MARRIAGE

For those of you not familiar with the term role, it basically refers to an individual's function or participation which requires certain behavior. For example, the man has the function or role of actually participating as a husband, which may entail being the chief provider of the family income. He also may function as the handyman, the cook, the bill payer, the person in charge of the automobile(s) and other mechanical things. Likewise the woman assumes the role of the wife, homemaker, second job holder, the children's primary caregiver, the house cleaner, the gardener, and the school liaison.

We all adopt roles in a marital relationship based on our beliefs, lessons from our families of origin, and whatever we negotiate with our mate that seems appropriate for our relationship. This can be very much a trial and error process, or it can be pre-planned prior to marriage and implemented temporarily or permanently.

There will also be times when roles may change based on altered life circumstances or changes in your personal perspectives. Make these decisions carefully and thoughtfully—together. In addition to the multitude of roles which get created, we assume the subtle roles of best friend, lover, and confidant. All of this makes for interesting and challenging participation in what should be a lifelong commitment to one another.

IS IT GOOD FOR ME?

This expression reflects an attitude in many young marrieds which should be reversed. "Is it Good for Her or Him?" should replace the first person emphasis if you are going to have a strong marriage. I am talking about filling the emotional needs of your partner, not just the physical or material requirements. No one can be all things to all people, and certainly none of us is a perfect mate. Truth to be known, few of us really expect our mates to be perfect. However, I must point out we can always try to be mindful of doing things that help fulfill the needs of our partner. Attempt to put forth the necessary effort to accommodate what's best for your partner on a regular basis, not once a year, but at least once a day if possible.

It is important to get feedback from your partner about his or her needs. Ask for specific feedback; it will provide the information you require to help give what your partner desires. Your partner, of course, must be asked to be honest and candid. Without that honesty you are less likely to be able to adjust your efforts appropriately.

The best way for you to get what you need is to find out what your partner needs; then do your best to fulfill those needs. Not only will you feel better about who you are and how you are valued by your partner, but this will create an environment where your partner will want to respond, reciprocate, and participate more willingly.

SELF INTERESTS

Husbands and wives need to have their own interests, hobbies, and friends who each pursues separately as individuals. There are times when we all need to participate in activities without our partners; to do something that we identify with only ourselves. We may be devoted to the "we-ness" in life, but it is healthy also to focus on the" me-ness" in life. There is no "we" without "me".

If you try to hinder your partner's times apart from you, it may have a destructive influence on the relationship. Also, dependency on your partner for everything you need is asking more than what most relationships can provide.

Your personal development is essential to the health of your marriage. It is through this developmental process that you can build and sustain self-esteem, self-worth, and expand who you are. If you value yourself, your partner will value you. If you strive to make to make yourself the best that you can be, it will likely lead to an enhanced marital relationship and will also motivate your partner to do the same.

WHOSE GOALS MATTER MOST?

His? Hers? Theirs?

Part of the process and purpose of learning about one another is to understand what aspects of life are most important. Prior to any discussions regarding these issues, I suggest each person make a written list itemizing, in order of importance and priority, your individual goals and marital goals as a couple. Once you've made your lists, you should compare yours with your partner's in order to understand their importance to your partner, and more importantly how the two of you can achieve as many personal and mutual goals as possible. This process may take considerable time, effort, flexibility, adaptability, and compromise. You must be honest with yourself and with your partner. You both need to be able to define and separate NEEDS from WANTS, and be realistic about accomplishing both.

WHO IS NUMBER ONE?

He is! She is! You both should consider each other as number one in your lives, forever. Oh yes, I realize there are times when the children will seem to consume your existence, but don't let those periods of time prevent you from being committed to your relationship with your mate. Always find the time each day to have private time no matter how brief that time may be. Always take the time each day to let your mate know how much you love and appreciate him or her.

SWAP ROLES FOR A DAY

Whenever a person does a job or task well, that job looks relatively simple and easy to the observer. This vie applies to almost every job, task, skill, or talent in most normal settings. It is pretty easy to observe someone performing his or her role and to judge the degree of difficulty—or so we think. The fact is that unless we have done the same job under similar circumstances, for a similar length of time, we really do not know as much as we think we do.

It is common, natural, and unfair to presume to really know what it is like to actually walk in the shoes of another person. In an attempt not to take your spouse or partner for granted, let me suggest that you swap roles or shadow each other for an entire day. This will enable you to gain a new perspective and a greater appreciation for the other person. If you can accomplish this, you will likely improve your relationship and have a greater respect for your mate.

AT THE END OF THE DAY

Every day that you are together, try to end each day with a smile, a hug, a kiss, a "thank you", or an "I love you". Never go to sleep mad at one another. Try to resolve disagreements, or at least temporarily agree to disagree. Don't let the sun set on an angry environment. At the same time, remind one another of your love and commitment to each other. Endeavor to work on the resolution of a problem as soon as possible. End your day with a prayer or a positive thought about the day and your appreciation for your partner. Sleeping with a smile is so much healthier than sleeping with a frown, both physically and emotionally.

CHANGE—IS IT GOOD?

It may be good, it may not be so good, but change will happen. It is important to recognize and understand that when one partner changes, whether the change is positive, negative, or somewhere in between, the relationship changes in some way. The pre-existing balance will have been impacted; any substantive change can disturb the balance. Do not deny change, but work with the changes as you work through the changes. Communicate with your partner about any change you are experiencing. Constant change is inevitable; it will require continual adjustments in the relationship. Keep in mind that successful adjustments require ongoing communication.

Remember that no matter how much we agree on things, and how many things we share in common, we are all individuals with different beliefs based on our backgrounds. See your partner's position or change as being different from yours, not necessarily wrong, bad, or unreasonable—just different.

SEE A PROBLEM FOR WHAT IT REALLY IS

When interacting with, and judging our spouses, we tend to attach symbolic meanings, perfectionism, and moralistic evaluations to practical everyday problems. Everyday tasks and chores should be judged on a simplistic basis. Think for example as though it were a friend or neighbor performing the task you are judging instead of your mate. The level of evaluation and criticism would likely be very different if you do this. Try to be less judgmental and more accepting of one another's individualism. Don't make a mountain out of a mole hill.

SCHEDULING STRONG DISAGREEMENTS

Be smart about when and where you have strong disagreements (fights). Of course there are going to be minor disagreements that pop up and must be dealt with immediately (or so we think). I'm referring to recurring "hot button" issues such as money, sex, children, chores, annoying habits or personality traits. These issues can be so large and so important, that you need to discuss, debate, and negotiate them at a time when you are both calm, rested, and have time set aside to devote to resolution.

This time should be viewed as an opportunity to reasonably negotiate your needs within the relationship. Be respectful of the other person's point of view and stated needs. Try to understand things from his or her perspective, no matter how difficult that may be for you. If you can repeat your partner's point of view to his or her satisfaction, then you probably understand. If you already have children or are planning to have children, DO NOT fight in front of them. They do not understand this process the way adults do, and they should not have to pay the price emotionally for your behavior.

GIVE AND TAKE

Giving another person what they need, and doing so on a frequent basis will usually mean that you will in-turn, receive much of what YOU need. Most of us are reasonable and at least sensitive enough to realize when someone is sincerely trying to do things that please us. In response to that giving, we will likely give in return. "You scratch my back, and I'll scratch yours".

EMOTIONAL BANK ACCOUNTS

We all have our own private and personal emotional compartments within our minds. We can refer to them as our "emotional bank accounts". Regardless of whether we are stingy givers or generous givers, we all need to supplement the withdrawals with deposits. We don't usually ask for the deposits to be made, or specify who should make them; but we definitely need them.

As a life partner, you should be making frequent deposits into your loved one's emotional bank account. These deposits almost never need to be large or grand; they actually fill the account faster if they are in the form of lots of small deposits. The thoughtful words and deeds that take effort, sincerity, consideration, caring, sharing, and appreciation make up those small deposits. Emotional bank accounts which are kept full will build strength in a relationship and keep the connection intimate; they really do pay great dividends.

HOW DOES YOUR GARDEN GROW?

You must tend your garden daily if you expect it to flourish and be beautifully productive. You must turn the soil, pull the weeds, and provide the water in order for the sun to nourish growth, and not parch. All of these things are necessary in order not to allow your garden to gradually die off.

The natural tendency for spouses is to gradually drift apart over time unless they work at staying close and together. Working the relationship means tending the garden (each other's or the community garden). It takes a conscious, daily effort to demonstrate how much you value that which your garden produces. If you sow with grace and gratitude, you will reap a life of love and devotion.

WHAT IS IT WORTH?

Could you place a value on your relationship with your chosen life mate? Maybe, but I suggest you find the words to describe how valuable you feel your relationship REALLY IS. Those words should generate feelings and emotions which will reflect your motivation to make this relationship your top priority. Every day in life requires adjustments in our behavior—behavior that WE choose. CHOOSE open-minded, considerate, and understanding behavior. CHOOSE to value yourself and your partner.

PRACTICE, PRACTICE, PRACTICE

What we practice most in life becomes habit to us! Both men and women need to discover the emotional needs of one another and gradually work out ways to satisfy those needs for each other. This can be very challenging at times because it may mean doing something you are not accustomed to doing. Listening not only with your ears but with your mind, your heart, and all of your senses is a challenge that requires effort, patience, and most of all, practice, practice, practice.

GRAB BAG ITEMS

In all aspects of life and in all of your relationships, especially with your spouse, try not to react too quickly to situations that occur. Develop a personal HOLD button. Put yourself on hold for a few moments and think before you react. This will allow you to consider an appropriate response rather than a hasty reaction. We tend to react before we think much more frequently than we are aware. This pause will become an enabler of control within us. Practice this technique often, it really does work.

Spend lots of time discussing the idea of living together before you decide to cohabit or get married unless you already know the details, or have already lived with your future partner. Learn what each other's preferences for lifestyle and home style are. Learn about issues such as neatness, cleanliness, organization, roles, chores, eating habits, etc. Little things about the other that irritate you or your partner can become magnified out of proportion and cause a split. It's great to love another, but if you don't like the little habits, idiosyncrasies, and personal realities of that person, they become objectionable road bumps to a lasting relationship.

It is reasonable to make the assumption that you are physically attracted to your spouse or partner. Hormones may help get us together but they are not likely to keep us together. Physical attraction is a realistic and normal part of a male-female relationship, but it should not be the single most predominant feature on which to base a long-term loving life together. Certainly you should strive for a physically healthy lifestyle that will help insure quality and longevity. Each of you will appreciate and respond to a mate who strives to retain his or her physical appeal for the other.

CONCLUSION AND OVERVIEW

For the majority of us, marriage is at best a trial and error process. Try to understand that planning and sustaining a life together involves looking at many different aspects of both "me" issues and "we" issues. The period of courtship and infatuation are full of attraction, romance, passion, pleasing, and togetherness, all of which are warm and wonderful. But those feelings naturally become somewhat subdued once the demands of life as a couple or a family set in. Life becomes more ordinary unless you have a plan to make it lasting and worthwhile. Marital exploration and planning will increase the odds of having a smoother and less stressful period of adjustment during the early years; and perhaps a more harmonious, enduring, and healthy relationship, which will endure.

Change is inevitable and growth is likely. Learn together about one another and make your marriage a priority in your lives. Educate yourselves by reading books, by talking, and by listening. Be open to counseling in the event the lines of communication become blurred or closed. Remember that life is not an emergency, move unhurried, diligently, purposefully, and passionately through the process of knowing, sharing, understanding, and appreciating each other as you experience life together.

Be each other's best friend, biggest fan, and most solid supporter. Always ask yourself: Am I contributing to the relationship with my behavior or am I contaminating it with my lack of thoughtfulness? Always remember that each day is a gift; celebrate life, living, and the opportunity for giving. Give to yourselves and to others.

SUGGESTED READING LIST

Love Is Never Enough
Aaron T. Beck, M.D.

Reconcilable Differences
Andrew Christensen, Ph.D. and Neil S. Jacobson, Ph.D.

How To Live With Another Person
David Viscott, M.D.

Complete Marriage and Family Home Reference Guide
Dr. James Dobson

Renew Your Marriage at Midlife
Steve Brody and Cathy Brody

Peer Marriage: Men and Women Gaining Together
Richard Mackey/ Bernard A. Obrien (textbook)

Kids Don't Come with Instructions

A Pocket Guide to Raising Children

by
Dennis Pezzato, PhD.

Buonsenso Press
Cambria, California

There is no roadmap available to guide parents and children through this process. It's no wonder many of us get lost along the way. I would like to give you some things to consider while on this journey.

Contents

Introduction

My purpose in writing this book is to share with you my opinions and ideas about raising children in a way that will allow them to develop into well-adjusted, responsible, and contributing members of society. Accomplishing this for our children is a difficult and often frustrating process. For the most part, parents are not given any formal training in parenting, so we use our own parents as examples and try to remember the things they did in raising us. After that we just sort of fly by the seats of our pants and struggle through the process. If we as parents are unsure and struggling, I have to wonder what effect these struggles (and related uncertainty) have on the children.

Perhaps if we can develop an understanding of some basic principles of human nature and socialization, then we can try to organize our thoughts and our own opinions, enabling us to put together a road map to follow. I believe that without an educated and purposeful direction, parents will not stay the course (if in fact there is a course) and the children can have little or no direction.

How to Utilize This Book

This is not intended to be a how to book or an all- inclusive text. I pose questions and share opinions and concepts for you to consider. I want you to evaluate the validity of what is stated and formulate your own view. I suggest you have conversations with your spouse, significant other, or whomever shares your child-rearing responsibilities. If you feel a concept has merit then decide how you would implement using it.

I encourage you to follow-up reading this book with others by experts in the fields of child and adolescent development and parenting. Get educated about your role as a parent so that you might attain a clearer understanding of this process and its effects on you and your child. When you have finished reading all or any portion of this book, please see my list of suggested reading at the back of the book. I have chosen these because I feel that they will be easy for you to read, understand, and most importantly, implement into your parenting practices. These authors talk in a language with which any parent should be able to relate and feel comfortable.

Nurture the
Mom and Dad Relationship

Parents should work on their own relationship, keeping in mind all the meaningful aspects of being a couple. Keep the flame burning. Remember how the two of you felt when you first began your relationship.

Parenting as a Team Effort

Parents need to set aside ample time on a regular basis to discuss each other's ideas about how they want to handle the issue of raising children. They need to find common ground, ways to agree on developing an approach with which both parents can live. Nothing is more destructive than parents disagreeing about how to handle what their child needs. For the sanity of each parent, the sake of their relationship, and the stability of the child, it is important to present a unified front.

Sometimes we have to put aside our egos and strong opinions to be flexible. This will enable us to work toward a common strategy in the best interest of the child. A child can sense when parents disagree, even if the disagreement is not displayed outwardly. Two parents who are divided will do more harm than good. One parent in charge with the other quietly in the background would be a better alternative if disagreement is unavoidable.

If you are a single parent, in most ways parenting will be more of a challenge because you will not have the support of your partner. You may have the support, however, of family members or other significant adults in your life who may be willing to assist as a listener or peripheral surrogate partner. This might be a person who helps out on an irregular basis. The main thing here is to proceed with your plan, so don't spend a lot of time second-guessing yourself. Be flexible and be patient with your self. Parents need not be afraid to fail. Each day and each task is not a test. Do your best to stay on a committed path, and if something doesn't work as intended, then try it again or make adjustments that you feel make sense. Much of this process is trial and error. Practice being flexible and adaptable. There is a process of feed- back between parents which will help prevent failure. This is part of the overall process.

In the Beginning

There are some schools of thought that feel a child at birth is like a blank canvas, that parents can create on that canvas anything they like. I think that may be true to some degree, but I feel strongly that children are born with a certain amount of preprogramming over which we have little or no control. We are all born with a certain temperament which affects the type of personality traits we have in life. I like to envision a child as a huge filter which collects much of what is dumped into it and allows other things to pass through it. It is said that traits plus experiences determine personality types. Providing experiences are our responsibility. Parents and society have significant control over what a child experiences, and thus control to affect personality outcome and type.

Having said that, I must also say that there is no doubt in my mind that the more good and positive things you put into that filter (the mind), the more you can expect good and positive things to come out of that mind. Conversely, the more bad and negative things you put in, the more you can expect bad and negative things to come out of that mind. We as parents are here to guide and influence in a positive way. Children are incredibly open and receptive to what we say and do as their very own living examples. We must model acceptable behavior for them to follow. I will talk about ways to do this in some of the following pages.

Our Goals as Parents

Our goals as parents are both selfish and unselfish. What are the things we do purely for the good of our children? What things do we do which are convenient or in primarily our best interest? Do we understand what our motives are in parenting? What are we doing for our children? What are we doing for ourselves?

Good parenting requires work and sacrifice. If we are not willing to make this commitment a priority then we risk short-changing the child. It is too easy to use the television, computer, child-care, or other neighborhood parents to fill time with our child instead of spending time with the child ourselves. There is no substitute for direct contact between parent and child. Children need lots of physical and emotional contact in order to feel needed, part of something, valued, and loved. The quantity of time spent is important but the quality of that time is more important. This contact is most important, during the first three or four years and of course remains important forever. Children need verbal affirmation and verbal comfort.

Our goals as parents should be to guide our children toward becoming responsible, contributing, and caring adult members of society.

Is Loving Enough?

The emotion of love seems to come naturally for most parents. Love is an emotion but also a commitment. It is a choice to provide structure and discipline—or not. Structure inherently contains the experience of love. Guiding that child with structure and loving discipline may be unnatural and very difficult for many parents. As parents we want to maximize our own enjoyment and minimize our stress while raising our child. We need to be committed to providing structure in his life, structure that he will incorporate and carry into adulthood. Many experts agree that the emotion of love is not enough; love without structure and discipline will not take root, will not last, nor will it be passed on. We are here to prepare our child for adulthood. Love alone is not enough.

What about Structure and Discipline?

Structure is like having a road map to follow as we wind our way through life. Structure is the way we define pathways, guidelines, and rules. Such structures and maps get incorporated into one's life and assist in defining one's identity and sense of self. It helps to determine how we fit or where we belong in the world. As parents we should want to make our child's road in life well-defined and easy to follow. We do this with structure and loving discipline.

Some of us confuse discipline with punishment. I consider them to be two very different things. The word discipline has its origin in the word disciple, or teacher. Discipline, to me, means teaching and guiding in a structured and organized manner. If a person is said to have self-discipline, then that person is thought to have the ability to live within certain structured boundaries. He has some degree of self-control. In my opinion discipline is a good thing. On the other hand, punishment definitely has a negative connotation, because it usually means someone was bad or is going to feel bad. I prefer consequences to punishment. Punishment can make everyone feel bad. We should try to teach our children through consequences. Punishment can damage self-worth and self-esteem and promotes aggression in children. Always take the time to explain the consequences of breaking the rules. The consequences of broken rules can be some of life's greatest teachers.

Rules are the backbone of any structure. Develop rules that are fair and reasonable based on age and level of responsibility. During early childhood, rules do not need to be very flexible in the sense that as your child questions or complains, you don't need to feel obliged to open a debate. Whatever you say, goes. Once a child reaches the age of reasoning (seven to nine years), however, you begin a continuum in his life where you need to encourage reasoning and thoughtfulness. This requires that you talk to your child more about the rules and their importance. Discuss fairness issues.

Respect the child's questions, and allow him a voice in formulating or adjusting rules.

Consistency
Compliments Structure

If we maintain consistency with the guidelines and rules we choose, our children will have simpler paths to follow and will understand what is expected. Structure with consistent application of expectations makes every person's role easier to understand and perform.

Children want us to provide structure. They thrive and are more self-assured when they know what is expected of them and what to expect from their parents. They experience structure as safety, which allows for more creative thinking and more ease in experiencing life's new challenges. Children feel protected and loved with structure in their lives. Such guidelines and rules applied with consistency become an emotional security blanket.

Teach Your Children Well

We represent the concepts of love, honesty, respect, unselfishness, and morality to our children. We do this not only by what we say but by how we conduct our daily lives and how we interact with them and with others. We are our children's most significant role models. We are their living examples of how to act as responsible human beings.

While teaching your children you must be ever mindful of how they view things. Try to understand their perspective on their world. Enter into their world and build a bridge to yours. Take them step by step to your world of love, honesty, and respect. Do this through verbal inquiries and living examples. Be patient and remember that you are an adult with a developed mind and years of living experience and they want to be like you.

What Is Quality Time?

Quality time is an overused term which is difficult to define and unique to each person. All time spent with your child should be quality time in some way. There is absolutely no substitute for the parent spending time with their child; it is essential. Try not to let your personal goals outside the home consume your time to the point of robbing you and your child of regular shared time and life experiences together. Regular and frequent time spent together is the basis for a fruitful family life and your child's personal positive development. Remember, time is precious and limited. Choose wisely how you use it.

More on Time Spent Together

A key element in our development and existence as humans is to feel needed. We—and our children—feel needed when we are included. We feel included when we are made a part of things. Spending time interacting helps to accomplish this.

Interacting can involve touching, hugging, and conversing (if age appropriate) and benefits both parents and children. Hugging your child is an expression of love and can instill a sense of self-worth in the child. When we are hugged we feel important, valued, and comforted. When we feel important our self-esteem grows. These actions, when lavished on the child, will also serve to teach him the value of doing the same to others throughout his life. This will serve him well when he is a parent.

A Little More on
Time Spent Together

Play with your children as often as you can. Play on the level they choose; try to remember what it was like to be their age and how much fun you had with age- specific toys. Try to relate to the children less like an authority figure during these short play sessions. This may create a different relationship between parent and child, one that may allow the child to feel a little more equal, temporarily, and see you in a different light, as a person capable of functioning on the child's own level and capable of understanding them and their world. Your child will see you in a different light by being able to emotionally experience you as part of their world.

Unless you are not willing to share something, let them make most of the little decisions during the play session. This allows them the opportunity to practice responsible decision making.

More on Play Time

Encourage the use of play toys and materials that enable the child to be creative and stimulate the imagination. Stay away from things that relate to violence and destruction. Playthings that challenge physical and mental coordination are positive and productive and should reinforce a positive self-image. Playtime is usually fun, but it can be so much more. Any time a child can experience the process and product of being creative, it should contribute to feelings of accomplishment and self-worth.

Alone Time

A person needs to get to know himself or herself, to be able to have uncluttered, non-social thought time. Encourage alone time, time for children to spend with themselves. During this time there should be no television, video games, or computer. Just quiet time alone. This concept applies to all family members.

During the early years pretend play and fantasies are normal and healthy, as long as they don't extend into adolescence or are not part of a withdrawal behavior. You should expect such pretend play and fantasies with young children. Playtime is when your child explores his world and all the objects in it. Imaginative play is normal and healthy. It is how we grow and how we exercise our minds. Fantasies and pretend play are how we develop and use our imagination, a key element in us all and a complete topic for another discussion.

Get to know the person inside yourself. Time alone can help us to look within ourselves, to experience our existence and how we relate to our physical and social environments without interaction with others. This time can help us formulate and ponder our individual perspectives and opinions and can provide solitary moments to explore our own thoughts without the constant reactions of others.

Preaching or Teaching?

It is important to be mindful of our methods of teaching children. Keep two key points in mind. One, we teach and influence as much by example as by intention. We are the leaders and the demonstrators in our own living classroom. Two, when we actually teach by intention, it is important to try to teach by deliberately showing, explaining, reasoning, and respecting.

Try not to preach. When you preach you probably come across as too authoritarian and in the child's mind you create a distance that could cause the child to tune you out. Preaching may also feel too aggressive to the recipient. Preaching may be experienced as disrespectful and may stifle individual thought and questioning.

Try to teach with a gentle approach, using a conversational tone. I realize this concept may be difficult for parents to implement, but it may produce a better result and create an easier relationship between parent and child. If you are a parent, think back to the time when you were first helping your child learn to walk. Remember how gentle, encouraging, positive, and patient you were? Use that same approach throughout the years of growth and education.

Always "seek first to understand" the perspective of the person you are trying to teach. Include dialogue by using questions and answers. Encourage feedback. Remind yourself and your child that there are no dumb questions. This process will enable the child to incorporate your teaching and make it their own.

More on Teaching

While in this lengthy process of learning, a child needs to be praised with positive feedback. Praise the efforts made rather than the outcome or results. Effort is everything, whereas outcome-based living creates potential harm and resentment. Recognize the little steps of progress, and don't save the praise for large triumphs which may not come in the short term or at all. At the same time, be careful not to over-praise at a time when it really is not warranted or earned, because this could create in the child a false sense of reality. What I mean by this is that children whose parents constantly praise every accomplishment may be overindulgent, creating a pattern which might not be supported or repeated by society. My concern would be that if your child sees himself in an unrealistic way, the outside world experience may be very deflating. An under-praising method may reduce self-motivation and determination.

Be positive and constructive with your criticism. Put it in the form of an idea which you share, an explanation, or even a question. Once again a conversational tone will usually obtain greater results from the child or listener. If presented in a respectful and helpful manner, constructive criticism is feedback for learning.

Begin the Daily Journey

Try to start each day with your child in a positive way by showing a smile and giving a hug. Try always to at least begin every morning being cheery and upbeat— after all it is a new beginning. Do this the very first thing before the day has a chance to get going, before you begin to deal with any problems, issues, or tasks. Parents often have to push, poke, prod, and otherwise force certain actions at the start of each day, and that can be a negative experience for all members of the family. Just a comment: If you guide your child with loving discipline, using natural and logical consequences, you should not have to spend your life pushing, poking, prodding, and debating.

Make time each day for the entire family to be together. This could be at the breakfast table, the dinner table (my favorite), or in the evening before bedtime. On a hectic day, you should at least gather for a group hug and a positive statement about the day or some part of the day. Perhaps you could share a good thought or a short prayer. This can give a real boost to everyone and set the tone for the rest of the day.

Sharing this family time is important emotional glue. We need to promote a sense of togetherness and belonging. For children this helps promote self-esteem. When any of us feel a part of something, we usually feel an increased sense of self-esteem. The family unit is where this should all begin. Lives tend to get hectic, and spare time is hard to come by for many. Make whatever sacrifices are necessary to accomplish this regular time together to talk, share, and bond. Many families benefit from regular (weekly or biweekly) family meetings where issues, policies, and problems are discussed democratically. Children can learn problem solving skills, the value of give and take, and empathetic understanding of other people. They will feel empowered in the family unit.

Before the Work Begins

So much of what we do for our children in the name of love and responsible parenting during their early years may seem non-productive or
futile. Perhaps we feel we're not getting through to our children. To some
degree that is probably the case. We should expect delayed gratification,
because in reality the fruits of our labor will sometimes appear many
weeks, months, or even years later.

There is an old saying, "The fruit doesn't fall far from the tree." Of
course this could be seen negative or positive. Our children mirror us.
They emulate us without even knowing that they take on our behaviors
and attitudes. We all reap part of what we sow. Continue to do the things
you believe are right, and be open-minded about your approach, always
staying the course. In time the results will show. There are never any
guarantees in any of this. Remember to keep your goal in mind: to raise a
responsible, contributing, compassionate member of society. We must,
therefore, model and represent such qualities. You should be thinking
about what your adult child will be like after all the years of infancy,
childhood, and adolescence.

Keep This Thought in Mind

Always keep in mind that a manifestation of caring is sharing, and parents are charged with setting this example. Let the children see Mom and Dad display a sharing attitude both in and outside of the home, with family members as well as friends, neighbors, and strangers. We are the child's role models. We sometimes teach more by influence than by intention.

Whatever a child sees in the home is what the child perceives as normal. If inconsistency and chaos prevail, then that is what becomes normal to the child. If, on the other hand, the child sees consistency, organization, caring, and sharing, then that is what becomes normal, and that is what ultimately becomes the basis for your child's behavior patterns.

Love and Respect

We all want our children to love and respect us. I would like to go out on a limb here and suggest that if we do not abandon, abuse, or desert our children, our children will almost certainly love us. The attachment a child feels toward a parent, regardless of the quality of the parent, is unbelievably strong. Just ordinary parenting is sufficient to promote and maintain this attachment.

Respect may be a different matter. If we want respect, then I think we need to earn that by our actions and by showing respect toward our children. They are individuals with feelings, wills, intellects. No matter a child's stage of life, he or she has an individual personality, attitude, perspective, etc. Never fail to recognize and respect that fact. Parents who create an environment of loving discipline, who promote and live by rules which are fair and respectful, and who say what they mean and mean what they say are likely to have the respect and ultimate appreciation of their children.

Love is a result of the bond between parent and child. Respect cannot be assumed but must be earned, developed, and maintained. Respect is the foundation for all parenting practices. We must establish this foundation from the beginning of the parenting process.

Parenting—A Work in Progress

If we believe in the need and in the benefits of structure in a child's life, then there must be discipline. Do not be afraid your child won't love you if you discipline him. The child may not like you all the time he is being made to toe the line or accept consequences, but that dislike will pass. Stay the course with discipline and partner that with love and understanding.

Always try to communicate to the child that an individual act does not define a person, although he may need correction or consequences for a particular misdeed, it was the act of doing the deed you are addressing and not the worth of the person. To put this into simpler terms, I can do a stupid thing but that does not mean that I am a stupid person. Remember that we all make mistakes—lots of them. Mistakes can be educational for us. When we make a mistake we need to admit the mistake to ourselves, our partner, and our children. We should step back and try to see how we can improve on that particular behavior or attitude. Then it is time to move forward with a positive resolve that attempts to correct the behavior. All of this stresses the importance of the child himself. This will help to build and support self-esteem.

Practice Makes Perfect

Whether they are good or bad, the things we practice most are the things we develop as habits. The more something becomes a habit, the more normal it seems and the easier it is incorporated into our lives. Practicing sharing, caring, manners, cleanliness, organization, etc., tends to develop these traits into habits. These habits can evolve into what becomes our normal behavior.

Let's take manners as an example. I believe good manners are part of a foundation for learning respect for others as well as for oneself, thereby creating good social relationships. Parents should teach manners at an early age, as soon as the child starts talking. You should insist on good manners in all settings. Remember that practicing manners is a two-way street. Parents need to display manners to their children if they expect the children to value and develop good manners. The practice of good manners almost guarantees an increase in self-esteem. We are our children's example. Children will not do as we say but will do as we do. Once your children experience adults outside the home and display the good manners practiced at home, they will feel good about themselves because those adults will almost certainly take notice of that behavior and will probably be complimentary of the child's high degree of respect.

Children and
Their Contributions

Children are part of the family unit and should be required to contribute to the family setting. Giving children responsibilities of their own teaches them to be part of the unit, which in turn makes them feel valued and needed. This may also help to instill in them a sense of pride in the contribution they made as well as in the family itself. For example: A three-year-old can grab groceries off the shelf at the market and put them in the shopping cart. A five-year-old can clear the table after meals, empty the wastebaskets, and sort the recycle items. A seven-year-old can dust furniture, sweep floors and walkways, help cook meals, and feed animals. A ten-year-old can wash the car, wash windows, and care for pets. All children can keep their rooms clean and picked up at a level befitting their age.

Ask for your child's opinion about things you choose for them to do. Try to act on the opinion if it seems reasonable. This approach is more likely to make them feel they are making a contribution. If children do not participate by contributing, they will probably become takers and not givers. If you allow your children to become takers in life, then I believe you will grow to regret your choice, and society will be worse off because of that.

Our goals should be to have a happy and mentally healthy family experience now and in the future. Parents who raise their children in a positive and responsible way will probably enjoy the fruits of their labor later in life when their children have families of their own. Whenever we make a contribution to anyone or any thing, we are giving of ourselves. When we give of ourselves, there is usually internal self-recognition and frequently external recognition from others. The result is almost always a feeling of self-worth and increased self-esteem.

Chores—
That Dreaded Word

Chores, no matter how small, should be assigned at a very early age. Age three or four is not too young for a child to start making a contribution to the family unit. Doing chores on a regular basis can help to instill a sense of belonging and is the beginning of learning a work ethic.

Begin with very easy chores of a short duration of time. During this process it is important to place a value on these efforts and to communicate that value to the child. (Value here means that you appreciate that the child is helping.) Positive reinforcement in the form of praise and appreciation is absolutely necessary. Let the praise be the reward, and do not establish a pattern of material rewards for chores that are done. This sends the wrong message. You don't want the reward to become the reason for their contribution. The contribution needs to be viewed as a necessary part of life, and it should be its own reward. Rewards can and should be given for actions and performance above and beyond what you perceive to be normal. We must help our children move from external rewards to internal satisfaction.

As you move through some of these ideas, never lose sight of the fact that one of your main goals as a parent should be to prepare your child to function in the adult world with adult expectations and adult consequences. A child who has learned and practiced a strong work ethic will find the adult world much less intimidating and harsh.

Some More on Chores

The teaching and monitoring of chores can sometimes be very time consuming for parents, and there is a temptation to feel that it would be easier if the parent just did the chore themselves in order to save time. It is common to hear parents say "I don't have time for this. I'll just do it myself, and then I won't have to do it over after Junior does it." Stop! Do not give in to that way of thinking. Hang in there—it gets better and easier with time and practice. Parents who do take the easy (lazy) way out are doing themselves and especially the child a disservice.

What message do you send the child if you do everything for them? That they do not have to contribute? That you can do things better and faster, so don't bother trying? That you will always be there to do the chores and the tough tasks for them? You absolutely do not want to wait until your child is a teenager to get him accustomed to making regular contributions around the house. The process needs to begin early in life so that what they practice and get used to becomes natural and normal. Remember to be patient with their progress. It is the effort and not the outcome which is most important.

In time the outcome will get better. Besides, if you think teaching a four-year-old to do chores is difficult, just image the battles you'll have trying to convince a hormone-ridden teenager to do chores.

Earn While You Learn

At some point after you have spent four or five years teaching your child to make contributions by doing chores and helping out, perhaps around the age of seven or eight you might want to consider giving an allowance so that the child can have money of his own. This is a good age to start teaching about money and budgeting. Receiving an allowance is a big deal to a child, so it must come with strings attached. No chores, no allowance!

An allowance should be budgeted into categories (spending money, savings account, etc.). Each week so much money gets allotted to spending, so much to long- term savings for a big-ticket item, so much to charitable donations, so much for gift-giving to family and friends. I think you get the point here. Older children might get a clothing allowance.

Once again the important thing is to start teaching and implementing things early in life so they become familiar and routine later. You also need to follow up on teaching financial responsibility from childhood into early adulthood. Teach the importance of understanding how and when to use credit and credit cards. If you use a credit card, you should be prepared to pay the bill in full when it comes.

Many parents themselves do not know how to live within their means, but they need to break that cycle and change their approach. There are plenty of books that can help you revise your budgeting techniques. Money is power, and power enables us to have choices. Responsibility and proper financial training will empower your children.

Doing More Can Mean Less

Beyond a certain point (you define where that point is), the more you do for your children, the less they will do for themselves and the more they expect from you. I believe this is basic human nature.

The more children are made to earn what they get, the more likely they will be to respect what they have. The more they earn what they have, the more likely they are to feel good about themselves and their accomplishments. If something is worth having, it should be worth working for. If this is not the case, then perhaps we don't need or should not have that something.

I believe that we as parents can make the harsh realities of adult responsibilities much easier for our children if we do the right things early in their lives. Once our children leave us, they need to be able to fend for themselves. We must give them the tools they will need.

We have all heard so much about self-esteem over the last few decades. Self-esteem, self-worth, self-respect are all very important, but they are less attainable to a child who is overindulged by his parents. Self-accomplishment (doing for and succeeding for oneself) will lead to self-esteem and all the rest. Accomplishing age appropriate tasks will result in an internal respect for self. This will lead to independence.

Don't Spoil Your Child

Although our intentions as parents are good, there is such a thing as doing too much for a child. If you tend to solve problems for your child, eventually that overindulged child will become too dependent on you and will fail to learn problem-solving skills. A child needs to experience failure socially, rejection, and disappointment. After all, these experiences are in fact just reality. Let your child learn for himself what he can and cannot do for himself.

Don't give in to tantrums, whining, and obvious manipulation. Don't get me wrong here, it is normal for a child to continually push and push to try to bend the rules. On very minor issues it's probably fine to bend a little, but generally you must stand your ground and be firm. It's okay to be the bad guy—that is a parent's job. If you set reasonable limits and are consistent and persistent with the enforcement of those limits, you will eventually be seen as the good guy.

Be patient and understanding with the continual testing of limits which will naturally occur. This is normal, and it is part of the learning and growing process. Always follow through with decisions you make. Never make idle threats, because they will undermine your authority.

Children and School

Prior to the first school experience, parents should teach their children to have respect for authority. Respect in the classroom has deteriorated shamefully over the last few decades. Teachers, police officers, firefighters, and many others are doing a real service for society, and they frequently do not get the respect which they have earned and are entitled to receive.

Spend time being involved at your child's school and classroom. Get to know your child's teachers well. See to it that both teacher and student understand how important your child's education is to you. Let both teacher and student know how important that teacher is to you. We entrust the lives and minds of our children to the teachers in our schools. Stay tuned in to what's going on regularly.

Do everything possible at home to support and supplement what is done in the classroom. Communicate regularly with the teacher. Encourage your student to share with you the things being learned away from home. Take a sincere interest in what interests your student. Allow your student to try to teach you what they learn—you may find something you did not know. Try to get excited about education together.

Home School

Don't let the schools provide the only education your children receive. We are all teachers in the presence of our children. Teach them what they do not get at school, i.e. what Mom and Dad do at home and at work. Let your child follow you around for one entire weekday. It is important for him to see what you do while he is in school doing his job! Teach him your life-values by modeling those values for your child and with your children. Remember that they are always watching and listening when you least expect it.

I feel strongly that physical and moral sex education should begin at home, no matter how awkward or uncomfortable. Don't rely on the schools, playgrounds, and television to provide for your child's sex education. It is your responsibility. Learn how to present it, and just deal with it the best you can. Otherwise seek help from a healthcare professional or clergy. This goes double for drug and alcohol education.

Get past the awkwardness and just do it. Your children need you to teach them these things. You have more influence than anyone else in their lives. Show them how much you care, and deal with these tough subjects.

Leisure and Learning

Whenever possible you should expose your child to other cultures, races, and ethnic backgrounds. Try to take on an attitude of wonderment and excitement to help expand his (and maybe your) awareness of the diversity in our society. Read, watch documentaries, and visit a different place of worship or an ethnic festival.

Expose your child to as many types of music as possible at an early age (leave out degrading or inflammatory types). The joy of listening to music with a wide range of styles is very educational and can be very stimulating. Any experience, such as learning a musical instrument (or voice), can teach the joy of expression from within oneself. It also teaches self-recognition of the fruits of one's labor. A sense of teamwork is promoted when this is done in a group, such as a band or orchestra. The body and the mind are both at work.

Encourage participation in sports and other forms of physical exercise and fitness. In competitive sports you should encourage the fun aspect and not the competitive aspect. Some of these experiences take too serious of an approach to what is supposed to be a fun and healthy childhood experience. Effort is more deserving of reward than result. A winner is one who applies effort no matter what the outcome.

Watch television programming which can promote good values and positive thinking. Part of the problem with much of what we see and hear on television, movies, and radio is that it is pure trash. It is full of violence and sex and not presented in any responsible manner. This trash is not good for developing young minds. When you put good stuff into the mind you can get plenty of good stuff out, and when you put bad stuff into the mind you get plenty of bad stuff out. Young minds are impressionable, pliable, and eager to soak up what is presented to them. We have the responsibility of what is placed in the minds of our children.

Get Ready for the Hormones

The early to late teens can be a complex and difficult time for most of us. It is a time of rapid change and growth. Patience and understanding are critical. Physical, chemical, and psychological changes are occurring at warp speed. Attitudes spewing forth from a teenage bundle of hormones can dominate our existence.

This is a time when parents feel least equipped to cope with the variety of changes they are forced to deal with, and if you think you are ill-equipped, just imagine how caught off-guard and confused your adolescent is during all of this. Your goal is to be the strongest influence in your child's life, even ahead of peer groups. You can only do that by showing respect, understanding, and a sincere interest in knowing your child. You must continue to live with structure and loving discipline as the backbone to your program. Continue to give advice (carefully), even when you think no one is listening. Offer space and flexibility, and don't over react to situations. You do have a right to demand reasonable amounts of respect, civility, and courtesy.

Prior to adolescence try to discuss with your child the kinds of physical and emotional changes that will be happening so that he or she at least has a clue that something strange is about to happen. Try to convince your child that the changes are normal even though a bit confusing. Let them know that you will always be there for them. Remember, this period will be the beginning of the process of independence, but you are the parent and thus the responsible adult. Be prepared to have frequent and open discussions about developing sexuality. You should be the primary source of information instead of the peer group.

The Wings of Freedom Cometh

As your child expects you to allow increased levels of freedom, you should expect increased levels of responsibility from your child. Let your child know that they earn freedom through responsibility. You may have to force this issue a little, because there will be some resistance to this concept. Though being patient and understanding are a necessity, parents should not allow the adolescent to be abusive, disrespectful, unappreciative, or uncooperative. Parents are not doormats and have a right to demand simple courtesy. Conflicts and disagreements will occur, but courtesy must prevail. Conflict resolution requires courtesy.

Expect your teenager to do things you once did. If your prior acts were wrong, then that same act is probably still wrong today. Bad judgment knows no particular generation. Confront mistakes openly, honestly, and as calmly as possible. I say as calmly as possible because anger and agitation do not solve problems or keep lines of communication open. Discuss the transgression and move on to correct bad decisions that lead to bad behaviors. Do this together. Discuss the ramifications of a bad decision and whose lives it effects. Learn from what is past, and don't dwell on it. Move forward together.

As the Wings Grow

One of my infamous sayings goes like this: "Give them more and more rope, then pray they don't hang themselves with it." This refers to giving your teenager more and more space and opportunity to be independent and be responsible. If your teen does get hung up (make mistakes), and he or she will (we all do), then be forgiving, understanding, and loving. As a consequence, however, the rope must then be shortened until he or she earns more freedom by making good choices and demonstrating responsibility. Then you can let the rope out again with a watchful eye. It takes time for wings of independence to grow large and strong enough to be self-supporting and able to carry the weight of flight.

The Power of Peers

Never underestimate the power of your child's peers and peer groups. They are the hormone-powered gang that you should not fear—even though they seem to have more influence over your child than you do.

Be a part of your child's everyday life. You have a right and the responsibility to know where he or she goes and who they are with when not at school, home, or work. Meet the parents of your child's friends. Know your child's friends. Control the activities in which your child participates. Respect privacy, but if possible, know what is going on at all times.

If you exercise loving control with a respect for privacy and independence, and if you have done a conscientious job in the early years, you must now allow your child to exercise his or her own sound judgment. Whatever threatening or negative issue might develop can be worked through with reason, rules, love, and understanding. Communication is a vital requirement to avoid losing loving control. Having said that, I admit there are situations that are just too challenging and complex for some parents. At these times we must defer to a mental health care professional who can be objective and who has the skills to help each of us see our problems and guide us through resolution.

Charity Away from Home

Surely charity should begin at home in the sense that we all need to be giving and sharing with family members. Expressions of love and caring can be diverse, so teach your children as many ways to give as you can; explore new ways as well. The important thing is that we continually practice giving to one another.

Giving does not mean you buy a gift. Giving of oneself in small ways might mean remembering manners, simple acts of kindness, remembering special occasions, helping out around the house—the list is endless. When we are thoughtful and considerate, it demonstrates to others that we feel they are important to us and that their feelings are important to us. It tells them that we respect and value them. I remember seeing a bumper sticker that read: "Practice random acts of kindness." Smiles and good deeds can change the way we and others view the world. Most importantly, such deeds transform us.

Equally important is to practice charity away from home. Practice doing things for those who are less fortunate. Do these things as a family or individually. Do this at a level that you are comfortable with and which makes you feel good about the act of giving. Giving can build character and improve self-esteem as well as creating a sense of community and belonging.

Religion, Spirituality, and Tolerance

At the risk of offending some people, I am compelled to say something about the importance of society's acknowledgment of the existence of a Higher Power. I think that some form of religious teachings, organized or otherwise, some form of spirituality with a sense of community, is absolutely key to our ability to function as social beings. For many of us the ideal of a Golden Rule, "Do unto others," was first experienced through some kind of religious teachings.

For much of mankind, a person's faith in a God or a Higher Power is what gives us the strength to complete the journey through life. Religious teachings can help give us a moral code by which to live. Most religions teach a universal morality, such as tolerance and regard for our fellow men.

Lacking any religious or spiritual education, we at least owe it to ourselves, and especially our children, to instill an attitude of tolerance and acceptance of other human beings. We are indeed a universal family, and as such we must learn to live together in peace. If we don't teach these things to our children, then I'm afraid we fail them and we fail society.

Parents and Privacy

Mom and Dad (or single parents) need their privacy. Their bedroom should be off limits unless permission is given to enter. In addition, "off limits" teaches a child about appropriate boundaries. Children are also entitled to reasonable privacy as well. Parents need a place or space to be alone either individually or together, a place where they can speak privately about personal and family matters, a place for solitude. Time out for parents is a necessity and should be made a daily ritual. This will work to help diffuse troubling days, relieve stress, or just allow rest and meditation. Time outs with both members of a couple can do wonders for mutual release and may even provide an avenue for the couple to work on keeping the flame and their relationship burning—or at least flickering.

Money Matters

Financial matters are certainly one of the biggest causes of marital problems. Maybe—and this is just a maybe— if we expose our child to prudent handling of money at an early age, we just might be helping to make their lives easier during adulthood.

I touched on this earlier, but it is worth repeating: Teach budgeting at an early age. Give an allowance, and set up a budget that requires certain portions of the allowance be set aside for desired and required goals. Let me give an example. Set aside so much for a week's spending money, and when it is gone that's it for the week. The child will have to wait until next week to have more to spend. The rest should be set aside for saving to buy something special, charitable donations, or something for gift-giving at special times.

It is amazing how a child's self-esteem can grow when he or she is able to earn and save, not to mention feeling as though they have some control and- choices where money is concerned. Discourage the use of credit cards at all stages of your child's money education. Some time during the teen years you might consider letting your teen obtain a checking account. Teach him how it works and monitor the use of it. No credit cards yet! Probably during their junior or senior year of high school (you be the judge), especially if he or she has a job (which he or she should have by now), it is time to discuss credit cards.

When a credit card is obtained, it might be wise to just have one card for emergency purchases and easy record keeping. You absolutely should not allow the use of a credit card until your teen understands how interest and minimum payments work to keep us in debt longer than necessary. The safest policy is not to charge anything on a credit card unless you have the money somewhere to pay the bill in full every month.

Grab Bag Items

It is healthy for children to understand that liking or loving someone does not mean you always have to agree with what that person says or does. Never let your child think that he or she is the cause of an argument or problem between Mom and Dad, however, don't be afraid to let that child see you disagree on matters not attributable to the child. It's okay to disagree and even argue calmly as long as the child also witnesses a resolution or an agreement to disagree. Don't walk away from those situations without some form of resolution or compromise. If you cannot accomplish this, then perhaps you should settle the matter in private. The child can learn from calmly controlled differences of opinion. Allow the child to witness compromise—it is healthy.

Don't be reluctant to let your child be made aware of the kinds of hard work and sacrifice it takes for parents to provide a family with all that it needs to function and thrive. Children need to understand the unselfish effort that is required to be a good parent. Don't make the child feel guilty, just try to make them see that a family is a team and being a team member requires unselfish effort.

In all matters and in all of your relationships with your children and with adults, try not to react too quickly to situations that occur. Develop a personal "hold" button. Put yourself on hold for a few moments and think before you react. This will allow you to consider an appropriate response. We tend to react before we think much more frequently than we are aware. This pause will become an enabler of control within us.

Conclusion and Overview

For the majority of us, parenting is at best a trial and error process. The time to think about parenting techniques is before we have children. Discuss your views on how you think you want to raise your children and how that might be accomplished. Get opinions from friends who seem to be doing things right (in your opinion). Talk to family members who have raised children or who are in that process. At the very least, do some reading of books and magazines on parenting. When you think you have a grasp on things and you are ready to start a family, make a commitment to work hard and make many sacrifices(changes) to accomplish your goals as a good parent.

Having children can change your lifestyle drastically. Most experienced parents will tell you the sacrifices are well worth all the effort because the rewards can be endless. Many of your parenting skills will come from your own base of knowledge and intuition. Listen to your instincts.

Remember to take care of your own needs along with the needs of your children. If the parents aren't "together," the child will sense that and react to it. If, on the other hand, you are pretty much together mentally and physically, then the process will be easier on you and the child.

And finally, I cannot overemphasize the importance of Mom and Dad putting one another first as often as possible. Keep the relationship intact and at the top of your priority list. Remember why the two of you are together. Keep in mind that one day the children will leave the nest and there will just be the two of you, just as in the beginning. Make certain those years in between don't get lost.

Suggested Reading

Positive Discipline for Preschoolers (Developing Capable People Series)
Jane Nelson, Cheryl Erwin, and Roslyn Duffy

Preparing for Adolescence
Dr. James Dobson

Kids Are Worth It! Giving Your Child the Gift of Inner Discipline Barbara
Coloroso

Setting Limits: How to Raise Responsible, Independent Children by providing CLEAR Boundaries
Robert J. MacKenzie, Ed.D.

Setting Limits with Your Strong-Willed Child: Eliminating Conflict by Establishing CLEAR, Firm, and Respectful Boundaries
Robert J. MacKenzie, Ed.D.

The Encouraging Parent: How to Stop Yelling at
Your Kids and Start Teaching Them Confidence, Self-Discipline, and Joy
Rod Wallace Kennedy, Ph.D.

Grounded for Life: Stop Blowing Your Fuse and Start
Communicating with Your Teenager
Louise Felton Tracy, M.S.

The New Approach to Discipline—Logical Consequences: A Practical
Guide to Instilling Good Behavior in Your Child from Toddler to Adolescent
Rudolf Dreikurs, M.D., and Loren Grey

Take Back Your Kids: Confident Parenting in Turbulent Times William
J. Doherty, Ph.D.

Redirecting Children's Behavior
Kathryn J. Kvols

Love and Anger: The Parental Dilemma
Nancy Samalin

Too Much of a Good Thing: Raising Children of Character in an Indulgent Age
Dan Kindlon, Ph.D.

Stop Negotiating With Your Teen: Strategies for
Parenting Your Angry, Manipulative, Moody, or
Depressed Adolescent
Janet Sasson Edgette, Psy.D., M.P.H.

Adult Children
Don't Come with Instructions

A Pocket Guide to Learning New Roles

by
Dennis Pezzato, Ph.D.

Buonsenso Press
Cambria, CA

Contents

Preface

"We must continue to grow in our parenting roles just as our children must grow in their adult roles."

There is no road map available to guide parents and their adult children through the process of learning new roles in an all-adult relationship. Given that many of our adult-child relationships experienced a rocky road along the way, how much different will the new adult-adult relationship be? Are we prepared? I would like to give you some ideas to consider while on this journey.

"Love and respect your adult children enough to allow them to experience struggle, frustration, failure, and even rejection. These experiences are invaluable life lessons."

"Keep in mind that criticism and judgment can interfere with the learning process and create distance."

Introduction

My purpose in writing this book is to share with you my opinions and ideas about how to relate to your adult children in a way that will promote healthy, loving, respectful, and reciprocal relationships. Accomplishing this can be a difficult and often frustrating and disappointing process. For the most part, none of us were given any formal training in parenting, so we use our own parents as examples and never think beyond that. Likewise, we were not given any formal training in how to have and maintain an adult relationship with our grown children.

As it was when we were raising our children, we must fly by the seat of our pants and struggle through the process. If this struggle exists, the process may very well be a two-way street which includes parent(s) and the adult child or children.

Perhaps if we can develop an understanding of some basic principles of human relationships and socialization, then we can try to organize our thoughts and opinions, enabling us to put together either a road map to follow or at least a better understanding of the processes that occur as we experience these inevitable changes in our lives and in our relationships.

How to Utilize This Book

This is not intended to be a how-to book or an all- inclusive text. I pose questions and share opinions and concepts for you to consider. I want you to evaluate the validity of what is stated and formulate your own view. I suggest you have conversations with your spouse, significant other, close family members, and others who have adult children. If you feel a concept has merit, then decide how to implement the concept.

I encourage you, after reading this book, to follow- up with others by reading experts in the field of family relationships and other material on adult relationships. Get educated in any way you can so that you might attain a clearer understanding of this process and its effect on you and your adult child. When you have finished reading this book, please see my list of suggested readings at the back of the book. I have chosen these books because I feel they may benefit you in ways that may increase your understanding of yourself and others.

Quotes from the Author

For the majority of us, parenting was and is, at best, a trial and error process.

Parents should not expect their adult children to look in the mirror and see Mom and Dad—in terms of values.

One of the most basic and healthy goals to strive for with your adult child is to have the most loving, respectful, considerate, and understanding relationship possible.

We can choose to be givers, through behavior, action, and our caring feelings, or we can choose to be takers who are willing to receive demonstrations of love and caring from others without considerate sensitivity to reciprocate.

There is a difference between being supportive, available, and generous—or being a crutch and an enabler of irresponsibility and laziness.

Respect is the foundation for all parenting practices.

There will always be a biological connection between parents and children, regardless of the quality or intensity of that connection.

Human Relationships

It is my belief that relationships in life hold the keys to most of our personal-individual happiness and mental health. We owe it to ourselves and others to strive for the most healthy, positive, loving, sharing, and caring relationships possible with our family, friends, and those with whom we share our life.

We can choose to be givers who demonstrate, through behavior and action, our caring feelings, or we can choose to be takers who are willing to receive demonstrations of love and caring from others without a considerate sensitivity to reciprocate. A valuable relationship is based on mutual effort and understanding.

Love and Respect

Love is a result of the bond between parent and child. Some form of love as an emotion will almost always be present. Actions that display that love will vary from being non-existent to extremely demonstrative. A person can love another without liking or respecting that person's behavior. Respect cannot be assumed but must be earned, developed, and maintained. Respect is the foundation for all parenting practices. We should establish this foundation from the beginning of the parenting process; however, it is never too late to start having and showing respect for your child at any age. If we want respect, then I think we need to earn that by our actions and by showing respect for others.

Nurture the
Mom and Dad Relationship

Parents start out as a passionate romantic couple, just the two of them. The couple enjoys and works at developing all the meaningful aspects of their relationship. Their flame burns strong and bright. Do you remember how great that felt?

Some time later you became parents—perhaps more than once. Life as you knew it was changed forever. It is likely that your relationship as a couple changed as well, in some ways not to your liking. If you were wise and lucky, you worked at keeping that "coupleness" spark at least flickering, if not burning. You loved your child/children in as many ways as you could.

You tried to teach them all the "right" things. Before you knew it they were on their own and away from home, your nest. What do you do now? Is the coupleness still there, or do you look at a stranger opposite you at the dining table?

Whatever the state of your relationship as a couple, you must always work at making it better. This is the most important relationship in your life. Do whatever it takes to rekindle the flame. Help each other through the next phase of your life together. If you are no longer part of a couple or have gone on to create a new couple, you still have a responsibility to work at making your new relationship the best it can be. You may have new challenges because one or both of you may have adult children who are now part of a blended family. Always try to make understanding the center post of your relationship goals.

Ownership

For many of us there exists a little-known and seldom- admitted feeling of ownership for our immediate family members. We may feel that we own our spouse and our children. Certainly we have a biological and emotional connection to our natural-born children; we have an emotional connection to our step-children; and we have an emotional and physical connection to our spouse or life partner.

There is a significant difference between having a strong set of sensory and emotional connections to another human and having a feeling of owning another human. In general, ownership carries with it a stronger sense of entitlement and control.

If the person who is feeling owned senses too much control or unreasonable expectations being placed upon him/her, there will likely be a resentment felt toward the controlling person. If resentment develops and is sustained or grows, it can ultimately breakdown and destroy the relationship.

This feeling of ownership is a natural occurrence but can do more harm than good to a relationship. In reality we do not and cannot own any other human. We can own things; we can own our thoughts and emotions.

Our Goals as Parents

You raised your kids the best you could. You loved and cared for them, guiding them through childhood, adolescence, and into adulthood. During all those years there were times when you were aware of your goals as parents; there were also times when you had goals but were unaware of them. Perhaps you managed to fulfill some or all of your goals, but now that that journey has apparently ended and your child is on his/her own as a functioning adult, you still have leftover goals.

Given that the parent-adult child relationship must naturally be a different one than that of the parent-child relationship, do you have any goals (new or old) for the new relationship?

At this point goals may become blurred with expectations, so I will save that discussion for a later chapter. Let me just say that one of the most basic and healthy goals to strive for with your adult child is to have the most loving, respectful, considerate, and understanding relationship possible.

Entitlement

We spent the better part of two decades raising each child. We spent sleepless nights nursing, feeding, caring, reassuring. We spent endless hours coaxing, pleading, encouraging. We cleaned messes, we taught lessons, we provided a living model. We worked hard and made sacrifices individually and as a couple. We frequently put our child's interest ahead of our own. We loved unconditionally.

Many parents feel that all of this investment entitles them to be treated in certain ways by their adult children as a way of showing some appreciation for all that mom and/or dad did for all those years. This feeling of entitlement is not unnatural or unwarranted, but it may be misguided and unattainable.

It is probably safe to say that most parents did not become parents for the purpose of having adult children twenty or thirty years later who would be available and dedicated to repaying their parents for all they have done in having and providing for their children.

So are parents wrong to feel a sense of entitlement? I don't think there is a right or wrong answer here. What I do think is that it probably is not healthy or in our best interest psychologically to feel we have a right to or are owed something because of what we gave. What did we give anyway? How did we give it? We sowed, what will we reap? More on this later as we discuss expectations.

Is the Work Finished?

So much of what we did for our children in the name of love and responsible parenting during the early years may have seemed futile or non-productive. Perhaps we felt we were not getting through to them. To some degree that is probably true. The fruits of our labors emerge later in many cases—and in some cases not at all. There is an old saying: "The fruit doesn't fall far from the tree". This could be seen as positive or negative. Our children, as they were developing and growing, mirrored us. They emulated us without even knowing that they frequently took on our behaviors; much of the time we were not even aware of the extent to which this occurred.

It is likely that we will all reap at least part of what we sow. Keep in mind that what a parent has in mind to teach may not be perceived the same by the child who is trying (or not trying) to learn. Never forget that in the past as well as the present, we teach as much by influence and example as we do by intention.

Love Is Not Enough

Love, even when it is unconditional, is not enough. In order for an adult relationship to grow and flourish, it needs substance that will sustain it. This substance takes on many forms such as: commitment, which requires a steadfast pledge to put forth personal effort toward the betterment of the relationship; sensitivity, which requires warmth and understanding of another's feelings and needs; generosity, which has its roots in unselfishness and a desire to share with others; consideration, which is expressed as thoughtfulness with a true regard for others; loyalty, which means we display a faithfulness toward another despite adversity; and responsibility, which means we hold ourselves accountable to others for our actions and that we are dependable.

These are not just words that are said. These are actions and efforts that are required. We must choose to act and not just talk.

Parenting:
A Work in Progress

Once a parent, always a parent. We often wear parenthood as a badge; some badges shine while some may feel tarnished. As long as a parent is alive, he/she will always be a parent. We just define ourselves differently based on the age of our children and the stages we are experiencing. We must continue to grow in our parenting roles just as our children grow into their adult roles. They will always be our children, and we will always be their parents. We may have to learn to parent less at times. We have to develop a gauge of when to respond to need, when to listen, when to help, and when to be silent.

Doing More Can Mean Less

As is the case throughout childhood and adolescence, beyond a certain point (you define where that point is), the more you do for your adult children, the less they may do for themselves and the more they may expect from you. I believe this is basic human nature. The lessons we should have taught them early in life are that they must earn what they get; no one is going to hand things to them. If these lessons were not taught or learned, parents should not take up the slack for their adult children. Once our children leave us, they need to be able to fend for themselves. We should advise them whenever they request it; we might make suggestions when we are aware they may not understand the consequences of their actions. What we do not want to do is enable negative behavior and irresponsible decision making by providing what they can provide for themselves.

Working oneself out of a difficult situation gives one the experience and confidence to cross the next hurdle successfully, all the while gaining self-respect, self-confidence, and self-esteem. Love and respect your adult children enough to allow them to experience struggle, frustration, failure, and even rejection. These experiences are invaluable life lessons. Your adult children will grow stronger and more self-sufficient on the journey through adulthood. Who knows? Improved self-confidence may even benefit your grandchildren.

Don't misunderstand my intention here. I am not saying you should not do nice things or not be supportive. On the contrary, there is a difference between being supportive, available, and generous, and being a crutch and a enabler of irresponsibility and laziness.

Is the Teaching Over?

Parents teaching their children is a commitment that should never end. The manner in which the teaching occurs however, is quite different than it was during the non-adult years. Now it is an older adult mentoring a younger adult. There needs to be mutual respect expressed as a basis for this relationship. The parent demonstrates respect and asks for reciprocal respect. The parent as mentor needs to be available, supportive, and understanding of the difficulties a younger adult faces throughout adulthood. This relationship of teaching needs to be an open and reciprocal relationship, one in which the mentor is willing to learn from the adult child. Younger adults are experiencing life as a different world from a different perspective, and as a result also have much to offer. There is no substitute for experience and the wisdom that comes from many years of living.

The younger adult can learn so much from the successes and failures of the older adult. Both parent and adult child need to develop a mutual respect for one another with open minds and eager attitudes, regarding learning from each other in a spirit of giving, caring, and sharing. Keep in mind that criticism and judgment can interfere with the learning process and create distance.

Ready to Leave the Nest?

When the time comes for your young adult child to venture out on his/ her own, it should be a positive experience for everyone involved. I'm talking about the time when it is planned that there will be no return. Prior to this there may have been temporary ventures out of the nest for summer jobs, for schooling or college, for experimental purposes, or any number of circumstances. The final departure may be difficult and somewhat emotionally charged based on the young person's level of maturity and the parent's reluctance to let go, but parents should offer advice and suggestions about formulating a game plan to deal with important aspects of independent adult living.

The choice to leave should be the young adult's. The choice to stay and for how long should be by mutual agreement, unless the young adult is overly dependent and/or lazy and the parents just don't want to let go. In either of these cases someone needs to get real and force the issue. It is healthy and part of the necessary natural process for an adult child to be truly independent and self-sufficient and physically detached from the parents. Make this a happy time for all by being supportive, encouraging, and respectful of the young adult's right to fly away with joy and pride. It is both natural and common for a fear of the unknown and unfamiliar to be present in the mind of a young adult about to leave the nest, so the parents may have to promote the process when the adult child expresses a reluctance to leave.

The Maiden Flight

Parents should have been preparing their children for this moment since childhood by offering structure, loving discipline, and opportunities for encouraged accomplishment, love, support, and respect. It is to be hoped parents have provided a model for responsible adult conduct, honesty, integrity, and a strong work ethic. If many, most, or all of these things have been attempted or accomplished, the young adult will have tools to succeed with greater ease. If these things were not accomplished, there will be many more struggles and a potentially frustrating and sobering experience ahead.

In any event, I believe it is a parent's responsibility to sit down with their young adult in the spirit of respect and warmth to have a discussion about collectively putting together a written game plan of some of the most important and impactful things to expect and for which to be prepared. This is a very individual and case-specific area, so there is no one-size-fits-all approach to use. Unique issues and needs may emerge as part of any discussion. This is an opportunity for every adult child to make this right-of-passage a positive one and also for parents to give assistance and encouragement if it is wanted. Never force these issues. If there is resistance, back away and respect that. After all, it is not your journey.

One Way or Round Trip?

Will your child be coming back or is this a final exit? Will there be a revolving door policy or is the door slammed shut? At the outset, let me just suggest that you hold off on converting the empty bedroom into a hobby room for at least a year; depending on the circumstance you may want to have the remodeler scheduled for the day after Junior moves—just kidding. Every situation is different, so you must be your own judge of what is best for all concerned. Just remember that the idea here is for this young person to be truly independent.

It seems that there has been a trend during the last several years of adult children in their twenties and thirties still living in their parents' home. Some of these situations are based in real need due to unusual and/ or unfortunate circumstances, not the least of which include single parent young adults with a child needing assistance. Whatever your personal policy regarding open door and open arms, try to remember that these arrangements, with few exceptions, need to be temporary. The goal should be for the young adult to have a plan of how, what, where, and when to depart. I think it is absolutely critical that if your adult child returns home for a period of time, there must be an agreed upon set of rules to deal with issues of finances, chores, schedules, and everyday living issues shared by adults as roommates. Respect, consideration, sensitivity, understanding, and appreciation are a must.

Are We Really Empty Nesters?

Is it true? Are they really gone for good? Are we really all alone? Am I really all alone? There are more questions in the minds of most parents in this situation than I can list. Thoughts and emotions are rattling around inside us like clothes tumbling in a clothes dryer. We can be happy, sad, proud, worried, relieved, depressed, and jubilant all at the same time. Many of us, especially— but not limited to—mothers, experience some form of separation anxiety. This is normal and healthy as long as it does not become prolonged or lead to depressive states.

Many parents practically devote their lives to their children. Regardless of the degree to which you are involved and connected throughout the years of living with your children, there will likely be some pain felt in the letting-go process.

This is the time in parents' lives when you find out how close your own relationship with your spouse has been over this period of years when the kids came first or your marriage came last. Be open and share your thoughts and emotions; be sensitive and understanding with each other. If the flame between you has died, find ways to re-ignite the flame and rediscover each other. If the flame never died, crank it up and have fun. Never be embarrassed to seek help, advice, or support if you are struggling with these issues. Many of us are not aware whether we possess the tools to cope with life changes; however, we can all learn our strengths and develop new tools. This is just a new phase of our great journey, enjoy the ride.

What About
Single Parent Empty Nesters?

If you are a single parent of an adult child, you may experience all of the same things discussed in the previous chapter, but you will be experiencing everything alone. You won't have a spouse, mate, or co-parent with whom to share the experience. It could be more difficult at times, however there is no reason you cannot develop a support system around you that can make tough times easier and good times better. This system can be comprised of a significant other, family, friends, co-workers, church groups, support groups, and even professional counseling should you feel overwhelmed by negative thoughts and emotions. You should take great joy in this part of your journey and your child's journey wherever and whenever you can find it. Choose to focus on you and all the positive opportunities in your journey first. This life transition can bring new and positive opportunities. Some of these opportunities may need to be discovered by you through a deliberate effort.

What About
Remarried Empty Nesters?

If you have remarried for whatever reason and you are the parent of an adult child, you may experience many of the same things discussed in the two previous chapters, except you will be going through this experience with a partner who may not have been in your lives during any portion of your child's journey into adulthood. There is an inherent non-connectedness as part of the family dynamic. You must be sensitive and understanding to your new partner's feelings and actions; likewise, your partner needs to become aware of and sensitive to your thoughts, emotions, and needs as you proceed and progress through the moments of your new role on this new journey. Openness, understanding, patience, tolerance, and communication are critical in developing and maintaining good relationships with and between everyone involved.

Do They Hold
Our Future in Their Hands?

In a way the young adults of today, some of them our children, do indeed hold our future in their hands. The twenty-somethings, thirty-somethings, and forty-somethings will make decisions and participate in life-events that will have an impact on their parents—us. Our children will have a more direct influence on our lives in the future because of the parent-child familial relationship. This could be a positive relationship, or it could be a negative one; that depends on the individuals involved and how they behave in and outside of that relationship (refer to the chapter entitled "Human Relationships"). Many wonder how they will be treated by their adult children as they get older and have their own children and family responsibilities. How much contact and caring will there be? How will we be treated in retirement and in old age? These are serious and difficult topics for all to consider. They are concerns that should be discussed between and among spouses and family members. I will discuss this in more detail in a later chapter entitled "Expectations: A Two- Way Street."

For now let me just say that regardless of what happens with children and/or other family members, each of us are individuals and as such have to be responsible for making choices that give us control, as much as possible, over how we experience our journey in life. Steer your own ship. Do what you need to do for yourself; help others as often as you can; don't worry about what may or may not happen based on a hope and dependency on others. We never really know who we can depend on and for how long, at any given time. We need to behave in such a way that maximizes our opportunities for multiple relationships that are supportive, caring, considerate, loving, understanding, and reciprocal, so that we will always have others to turn to and rely upon when we can no longer do everything for ourselves. For this to work, one has to sow the seeds of giving in order to eventually receive.

DENNIS PEZZATO, PHD.

Religion, Spirituality, and Tolerance

At the risk of offending some people, I am compelled to say something about the importance of society's acknowledgment of the existence of a Higher Power. I think that some form of religious teachings, organized or otherwise, some form of spirituality with a sense of community, is absolutely key to our ability to function as social beings. For many of us the ideal of a Golden Rule, "Do unto others," was first experienced through some kind of religious teachings.

For much of mankind, a person's faith in a God or a Higher Power is what gives us the strength to complete the journey through life. Religious teachings can help give us a moral code by which to live. Most religions teach a universal morality, such as tolerance and regard for our fellow men.

Lacking any religious or spiritual education, we at least owe it to ourselves to maintain an attitude of tolerance and acceptance of other human beings, especially our family members. Charity should begin at home and with our loved ones. We are indeed a universal family, and as such we must learn to live together in peace.

It's a Whole New Ball Game

Parents must realize and try to understand that the complete departure of an adult child signals the start of something completely different from what once was an in-house parent-child relationship. Parents tend to want to hold on to and function mentally and emotionally in the past. The past is gone. It had a different purpose, and we had different roles. This departure means that many, if not most, of our thinking and behavior patterns must change in order to adapt to a new time in everyone's lives. There will be many changes in the roles of parents and adult children. There may also be a change in values, especially on the part of the adult child. Your child's value changes may not reflect your long held personal values.

DENNIS PEZZATO, PHD.

Changing Roles,
Changing Values

Probably the most obvious role change in the separation process which marks adulthood is that parents no longer have the authority they once had and the young adult no longer has to obey or be subject to that authority. What happens during this transition is that parents, on the one hand, have trouble letting go of the power vested in that authority, while on the other hand the young adult can't flee fast enough to be out from under the confining feeling that authority imposed. This separation process also may mark many changes in values, not on the part of parents so much but markedly on the part of the young adult who is eager to establish his/her own individually autonomous style of living. Sure, some of the parents' values are adopted and displayed; however, some are hidden below the surface and may not show until some time in the future. Still other values will be new or reworked versions of parents' values. Parents should not expect their adult children to look in the mirror and see Mom and Dad—in terms of values.

You Can't Tell Me What to Do

Parents can't seem to quit "cold turkey" when it comes to being parents. After all, this has been a way of life for so long. The idea is not to stop being parents; the part that is important to the newly independent young adults is for you to stop telling them what to do and how to do it. They have heard that stuff for so many years that at this point it nauseates and infuriates them. They want to do things their own way and are willing to make their own mistakes—assuming they believe they are capable of making mistakes. It's a parent's responsibility to let them have total control of their lives. Just be there for them as a support and don't distance yourselves. Make every effort not to be critical.

Mind Your Own Business

An adult child who displays an attitude of wanting autonomy and pri-vacy is experiencing the normal behavioral evolution of a person who is expected to become independent by his/her parents and who him/ herself desires independence. "If you want me to be independent, then don't tell me how. Let me make my own independent choices without you looking over my shoulder or commenting and criticizing everything I do." That quote is representative of the kinds of sentiments commonly expressed by young adults about to separate or recently separated. Unfortunately many adult children who have been on their own for years still feel this way to-ward their parents. What should parents do if this is what occurs? Read on.

Is This the Child We Raised?

Indeed it is, but the key word here is "raised," which is in the past tense. We need to live in the present and the future. Whatever you did to teach your children whatever values you intended them to accept, whatever plans you had for their future or how they would turn out as adults, all that has been done and is in the past. You don't get any second chances at raising your children. Now it is their turn to use whatever you taught them as they see fit for their own purposes.

Yes, this is the child you raised, but now he/she is an adult, his/her own person who needs a relationship with parents who will respect them for who they are and who they are yet to become. They need unconditional love and a supportive attitude. If they need advice, they know exactly where to go for it. It would not be realistic or fair to look into your child's eyes and expect to see yourself.

Don't Judge Me

One of the toughest things for humans is not to be judgmental of others. I won't go into all of the social psychological explanations of how, what, or why this occurs, but suffice it to say there is a difference between having and offering an opinion and being judgmental. If you are a parent, it can be almost impossible to avoid being judgmental. You (and all of us probably) spent all of the child-rearing years being judgmental; how could you carry the burden and privilege of shaping a life without judgment? I don't have the answer to that, at least not a simple or short one.

Whatever was before can be different in the future. We are all capable of change if we are sufficiently motivated. If we need to make adaptive changes to ensure a healthy, more positive adult relationship with our off-spring than we should do that. There is a quote that states: "Nothing happens until the pain of remaining the same is greater than the pain of changing."

The subject was personal growth. We all should continually strive for personal growth. Choosing to be less judgmental with others is a form of personal growth. One does not have to compromise one's values to be less judgmental.

The Birth of a
New Relationship

Every day is a new opportunity to change your perception of reality. As the day approaches when you and your adult children realize that the great break and final cord-cutting is eminent, you should begin to prepare yourself for another birth in the family: the birth of a new relationship between you and your eager adult child. This should be an exciting time for everyone, even though there are many mixed emotions floating all over. If you treat them as children they will likely resent you and distance themselves from you. If you treat them as you would treat your very best friend, you may experience a bond unlike you ever expected.

Building Bridges

Bridge building in the physical sense is a calculated, methodical, purposeful creation that has as its ultimate goal a structure of strength and beauty. This same concept applies to the opportunity you have with your adult children if you choose to avail yourself of that opportunity. The building blocks for this bridge are the same for both parent and child, but the parent must take the lead. Those building blocks are things like respect, understanding, acceptance, loving, liking, warmth, caring, sharing, consideration, sensitivity, and communication. This bridge will allow you to cross over to your adult child's world, even though you will not always be involved in every part of that world. Remember, you are no longer entitled to be a part of their world except by invitation.

Just Friends or More?

We reap what we sow. We sow good parenting principles and, we hope, reap a good outcome. As individuals, however, we have no real control over another individual unless that control is granted to us. We should not want to control our adult children but only to influence them in ways we feel is beneficial to them and the relationship between us. There will always be a biological and emotional connection between parents and children, regardless of the quality or intensity of that connection. Each of us can choose our own behavior but cannot choose the behaviors of our adult children. Any healthy and mutually satisfying relationship takes effort. We can be friends to our children and friendly with our children, and we can be more. The more can be "best friends" or it can be a combination of friend, fan, learning mates, and soul mates—everything is possible.

What Hurts the Most?

Why aren't our children interested in our lives or in us? One possible answer to that question is that maybe they do care and are interested in their own way. "Well if they are, they have a strange way of showing it." The obvious retort to that statement is that it is up to them to show they care in whatever way they choose. It is not up to us to dictate the terms of how they treat us. We are not and should not feel entitled to that kind of control. Is it right, is it acceptable, is it loving? Everyone has his or her own interpretation of appropriate treatment. This is where the key word "expectation" plays a huge role in our relationships with everyone, not just our adult children.

Who Needs What?

There may be a process at work here that evolves in its own natural way regardless of our wishes. Parents often (too often) have an ongoing need to actively parent well into their children's adult years and further. Adult children seem to go in the opposite direction of proving their independence and lack of need for any parenting; this period of time can have as its hallmark a certain degree of insensitivity and/or disregard for the feelings of others—namely their parents. This may be what commonly occurs, but it does not have to happen; indeed it should not happen between loved ones. This tends to change when the young adults become parents themselves and deal with issues later in life, but this may all happen a little to late for Grandpa and Grandma's benefit. Parents need and want respect, remembrance, consideration, and regular contact. Adult children want respect, privacy, detachment and attachment, support when requested, and acceptance. Egos, false pride, and ownership aside, there is no reason why everyone can't have most or all of what they need in what should be a win-win situation. Each of us can make the appropriate choices to make this happen. We'll take a look at some ways to make this happen in another chapter.

Expectations:
A Two-Way Street

Expectations from either direction can result in disappointment if what is expected is not communicated. Don't get me wrong, communication is not all it takes to have one's expectations fulfilled—far from it. Communication is a cornerstone of all relationships, and without it there can be no satisfaction.

Fruitful communication is born out of the desire to listen and to be heard. Talk is cheap; meaningful conversation and an exchange of ideas, thoughts, and emotions require effort and commitment. We owe this kind of commitment to ourselves and to one another.

It is natural and normal to have expectations of those with whom we have relationships. Some, if not many, of our expectations, however, may not be met because the other person may not know that the expectation exists or may not agree with the reasonableness of the expectation. How do we go about sharing our needs, wants, and expectations? Easy. We talk, talk, talk, and then talk some more (nothing easy about it). I am a firm believer in family meetings while raising children. These can be semi-formal or informal but need to be regular and primarily democratic. These meetings give each family member a forum for full participation and a real opportunity to be heard. I think that this idea can work for parents and their adult children as well. Obviously things are different because each person is an adult. The important aspect of occasional adult family meetings is that each person has an opportunity to share what is in their minds and hearts to see how their perspective can mesh with the perspectives of parents and siblings.

No one is a mind-reader. If you feel you have a right to expect to be treated in a certain way by someone, you must express your wishes or accept the consequences of your choice not to communicate. There are no guarantees that after you do all the things suggested above everything will work out to your liking; life just doesn't work that way. Life is not always fair, but we cannot get even a little of what we want unless we go after it in a positive, honest, fair, and sensitive manner, all the while showing a willingness to take the first step toward a mutual give and take relationship with others. Unfulfilled expectations can cause frustration, disappointment, heartache, hard feelings, and distance. Don't go there, and try not to sweat the small stuff.

Appreciation and Reciprocation

One of the things that makes our world of emotional well-being go around is feeling appreciated for the things that we do for others. Appreciation is felt by the giver as a form of acceptance, a form of feeling needed, a form of self-worth. A basic human emotional need is acceptance. A basic emotional fear is rejection or failure. When we do nice, kind, thoughtful things for others but get either little or no reciprocal treatment, we feel sadness, disappointment, betrayal, rejection, and a host of other emotions. Those who try to live by the Golden Rule, "Do unto others as you would have them do unto you," have the expectation, for the most part, that the other person will reciprocate. It is critical that we all realize how important it is to do for others and to actively, outwardly, and frequently express our appreciation to others whenever they do something for us. We all need this; we all should do this; we all can do this; some of us just need to practice doing this more. Remember that what we practice most in life is what becomes habit.

I believe this issue, when applied to parents with adult children (and believe me it can work the other way around as well), is one of the most significant sources of heartache and disappointment experienced at this stage of their lives. Many parents feel as though they gave to their child before adulthood and planned to continue giving throughout their child's adulthood as well; however, the perception may be that the giving is not being appreciated because it is not being returned or reciprocated. Based on my research, this is the rule rather than the exception.

A View on Some
Young Adults—And More

At the risk of sounding biased or of offending others, I share with you my observations and opinions regarding the evolution of the socialization process that has brought us to the present point of having a society filled with many, not all, young and middle aged adults who are so self-absorbed that they are not aware and/or do not care how they interact with others, including and especially their parents.

It is well known by the masses in our society that the older and the elderly are less valued than at any time in our history. Youth is "where it's at." That being said, however, if this is true, then it is likely a by-product of our self-centeredness and preoccupation with ourselves.

I was born in 1944, two years before what is considered the start of the "baby boomers" (those born between 1946 and 1964). I am part of those children of the 50s and 60s, when the mantras often heard were "I need to do my own thing," "Give them their space," "Hey, man, that's not my problem," "I just need to find myself." I wonder why President John F. Kennedy implored Americans to "Ask not what your country can do for you, ask what you can do for your country"? If we have evolved socially to this point of self-absorption on the parts of many adults, and I am convinced we have, then what does this mean for parents of adults and older adults in general? It means that we should expect to feel ignored, disrespected, unappreciated, and very sadly disappointed. What can we do to change things, if anything at all?

What Do We Do Now?

We can begin by looking inward at our feelings and expectations of others; are we being fair. Are we expecting too much, are we putting our noses where they don't belong, are we respectful of others, are we giving what we expect in return?

Then we can seek to understand the other person's perspective, the other-person's world, the other person's realities. We can communicate by sharing our ideas, thoughts, and feelings. At the same time we must practice becoming the best listener we can; that is what we owe to the other person and to ourselves.

And finally we can try to be realistic in our expectations of others. We cannot control what is external or outside of ourselves. We can control what is internal, inside of us. We choose our own behavior, always. If things, circumstances, or relationships aren't measuring up to our expectations and we've exhausted all reasonable measures to understand, accept, and compromise, then we must find a way to adapt to each situation. We can choose to accept what we cannot change and adjust our behavior accordingly. If we agonize, worry, become depressed, and choose to be anxious about things we cannot change, then we do ourselves a disservice by wasting time, energy, and emotion; we rob ourselves of precious moments to enjoy life.

Life starts with the individual who must first find centeredness and fulfillment based on self-worth and a positive internal perspective. It is not productive or fair to judge one's own self-worth based on the actions of others. Life is first and last an individual's journey. Give and get the most there is available to you and keep moving forward. Remember that we choose our own behavior, we have a choice in everything. Look in your mirror and see life, love, and opportunity.

Quotes from
Parents and Adult Children

"One of my children does not respect himself enough to appreciate the foundations laid for him."

"I treasure the remembrances like thank you notes, birthday cards, phone calls."

"I see my role as a parent to appreciate what they [kids] are doing, give advice only when asked, and encourage them as needed."

"I try to be a good example of keeping a good relationship with my elderly parents, even though it is very trying at times, so that my grown children will see what is important."

"I give my grown children their space and let them know I'll be there for whatever they need; sometimes I'll say no in order not to be an enabler."

"I learn something from my children every time I am around them."

"From my father I learned what not to do and how not to act."

"The only way I can teach my children at this point is by example; hopefully our children will always be learning from us and respecting and loving us."

"We talk about everything with our children, old age, what we may need."

"The obstacles between us are misunderstandings, only talking it out will solve it."

"I think my children owe me courtesy—birthday cards, thank you notes, and Thanksgiving dinner."

"I love talking to older people and hearing their stories. I like to play twenty questions."

"I try to overlook the negative stuff with my elderly parents and remember that they won't be here forever."

"Sometimes my parents still treat me like I'm twelve."

"I think that roles are reversed now, and I need to take care of my parents."

"My son is in his own little world until he needs something. We seldom get cards or phone calls or visits on occasions that are special to us."

"We never discuss expectations. We don't know what they need and they don't care what we need."

"I would like respect and a phone call once a week."

"Being able to communicate in today's world, it is hard to see eye-to-eye."

"I wish my mom would be less critical and let me make my own decisions without trying to push me in an- other direction."

"Sometimes I feel like I'm twelve instead of twenty-one because she crosses the line regarding my privacy."

"Their expectations about my choice of a mate are obstacles in our relationship."

"Sometimes my feelings are hurt by my adult child's selfish attitude."

"My son and his wife have told me that being around me was something they did not want, so I seldom see my granddaughter. They'll come around when they're ready, so I'll leave the door open. It's hard."

"My mother (eighty years old) is always very negative, and she peaches. I dislike it, but what can I do? I won't abandon her, I'll just spend a little less time with her."

"I wish our kids would show us respect and love. What did we do wrong?"

"I try to stop by or call almost every day because I know it means so much."

Grab Bag Items

It is okay to disagree and even argue as long as there is a resolution or an agreement to disagree.

Don't make your adult children feel guilty. Just try to convince them that the adult family should still be a team and being a team member strengthens the family unit and requires unselfish effort.

In all matters and in all of your relationships with your children and others, try not to react too quickly in situations that occur. Develop a personal "hold" button. Put yourself on hold for a few moments and think before you react. This will allow you to consider an appropriate response. We tend to react before we think much more frequently than we are aware. This pause will become an enabler of control within us. Practice this technique often; it really does work.

Conclusion and Overview

For the majority of us, parenting was and is at best a trial and error process. Sometimes it is wise to step back from situations and place yourself into the other person's shoes to gain insight and understanding about their world and their perspectives. Build a support system of family, friends, church or social groups, and others where you have opportunities to share experiences and perspectives. Educate yourself by reading books and articles that may be relevant to your areas of concern. Be open to the idea of counseling for yourself and/or family members if things seem too difficult for you to cope with. Finally, if you are a married couple or life partners who have adult children, I cannot overemphasize the importance of the two of you putting one another first as often as possible.

Keep the relationship intact and at the top of your priority list. Be each other's best friend, biggest fan, and most solid supporter. There may be times when life boils down to just the two of you, so choose to cherish and enjoy each day together. When it comes to your children, try to attain the healthiest relationship possible, whatever that is. Always ask yourselves: Am I contributing to the relationship, or am I contaminating the relationship by my behavior? Remember always that each day is a gift. Celebrate life, living, and the opportunity for giving—to yourself and to others.

Suggested Reading List

When Our Grown Kids Disappoint Us
Jane Adams, Ph.D.

*I'm Still Your Mother: How to Get Along with Your
Grown-Up Children for the Rest of Your Life*
Jane Adams, Ph.D.

Get Out of Your Own Way
Mark Goulston and Philip Goldberg

The Power of Empathy
Arthur P. Ciaramicols and Katherine Ketcham

How to Live with Another Person
David Viscott

Getting Through to People
Jesse S. Nirenberg, Ph.D.

The Language of Choice Theory
William Glasser and Carleen Glassen

The Power of Apology
Beverly Engel

Life on the Edge (See Chapter Nine)
Dr. James Dobson

Contemporary Grandparenting
Arthur Kornhaber, M.D.

General Conclusion

Believe it or not, we are all gamblers in life. I say that because for every one of us, life is all about trial and error; that sounds like gambling to me. As a gambler, wouldn't you like to improve your odds of succeeding? Well, that's what improving your life skills is all about; the more skilled you become in all of the roles you play in life, the greater your odds will be for success. The added benefit of this perspective is that you will definitely experience more JOY and less STRESS.

Successful attainment of your personal goals in life, is really all about your personal behavior, your attitude, and the choices you make. Always remember that each day is a gift to us; celebrate life, living, and the opportunity for giving.

To Order any of these Books:

We Don't Come With Instructions: A Pocket Guide To Understanding Ourselves

Money Doesn't Come With Instructions: A Pocket Guide To Personal Financial Behavior

Marriage Doesn't Come With Instructions: A Pocket Guide To Planning A Life Together

Marriage Doesn't Come With Instructions: A Pocket Guide To Sustaining A Marriage

Kids Don't Come With Instructions: A Pocket Guide To Raising Children

Adult Children Don't Come With Instructions: A Pocket Guide To Learning New Roles

Contact:

Dennis Pezzato, PhD.
P.O. Box 1434
Cambria, CA. 93428

Website: www.dennispezzato.com

www.ingramcontent.com/pod-product-compliance
Lightning Source LLC
Chambersburg PA
CBHW060251100426
42742CB00011B/1713